Books are to be returned
the last day

START
SCULPTING

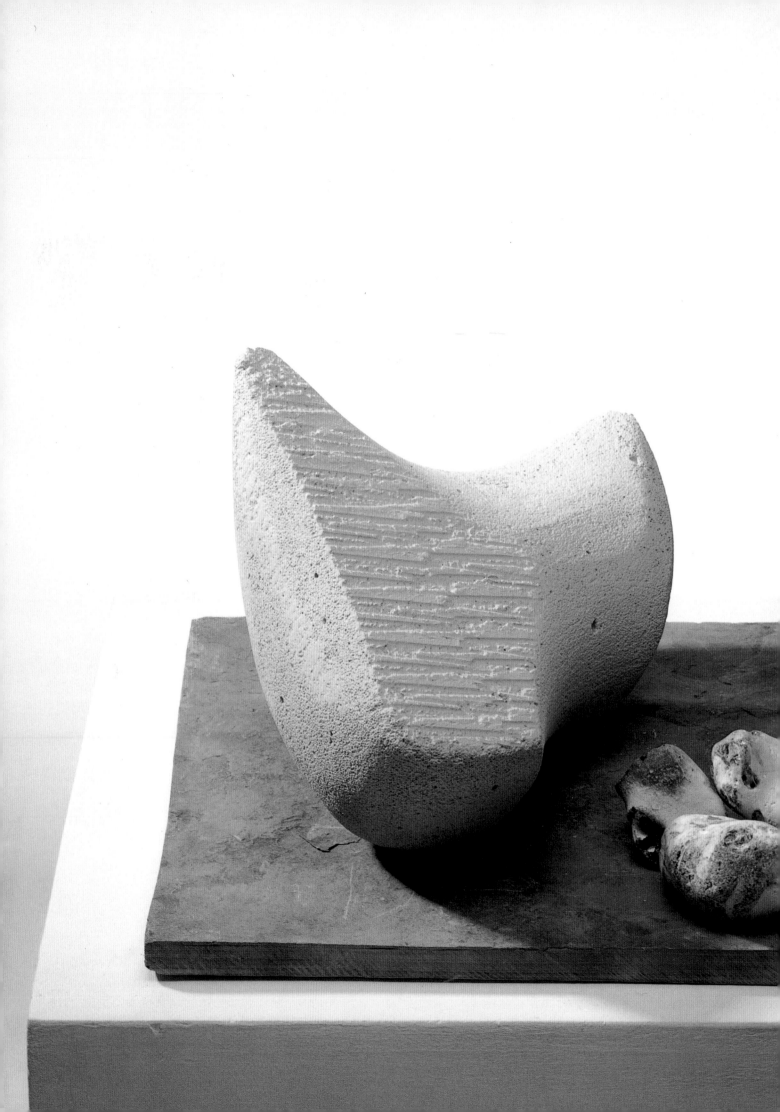

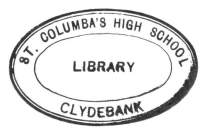

START SCULPTING

A step-by-step beginner's guide to working in three dimensions

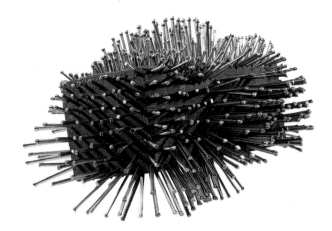

John Plowman

Quantum
Books

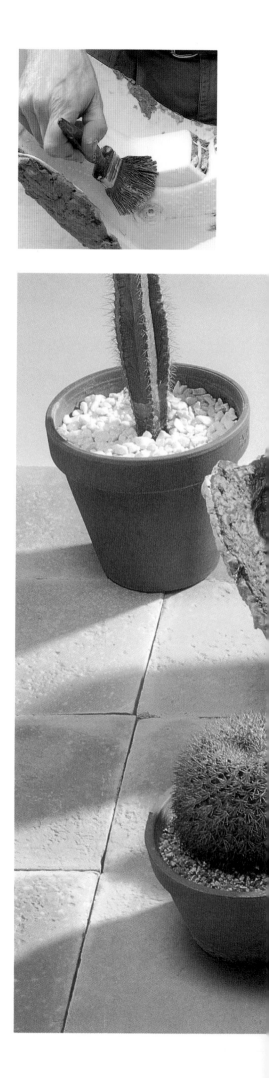

A QUANTUM BOOK

Produced by
Quantum Publishing
6 Blundell Street
London N7 9BH

Copyright ©MCMXCV

This edition printed 2000

ISBN 1-86160-393-2

QUMSCP

Printed in Singapore by Star Standard Industries (Pte) Ltd

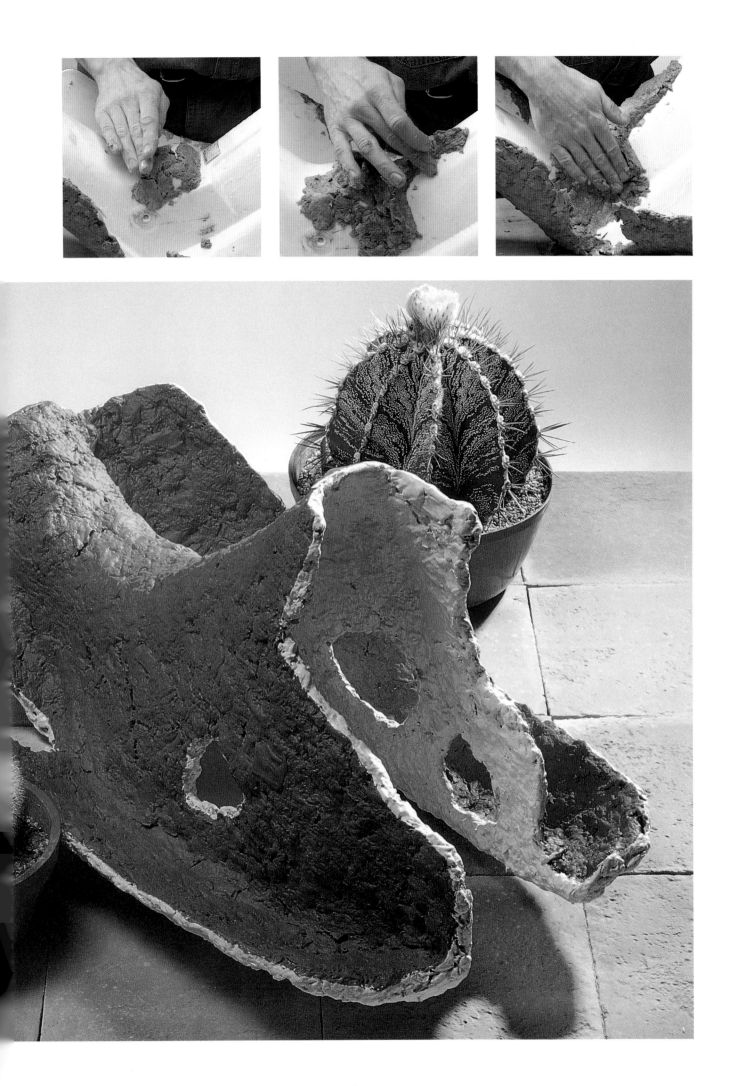

CONTENTS

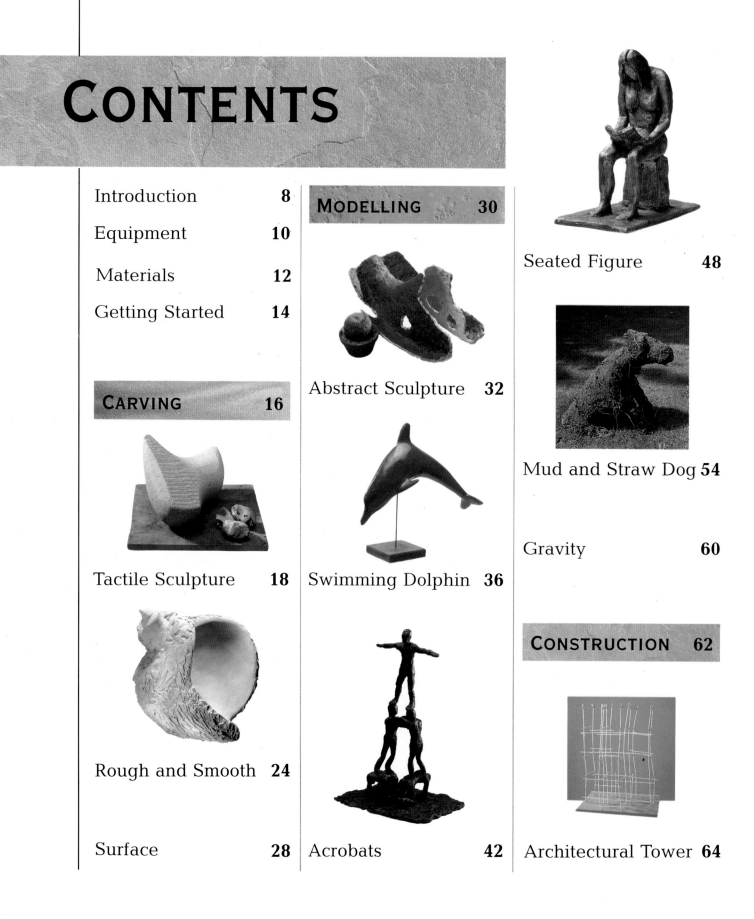

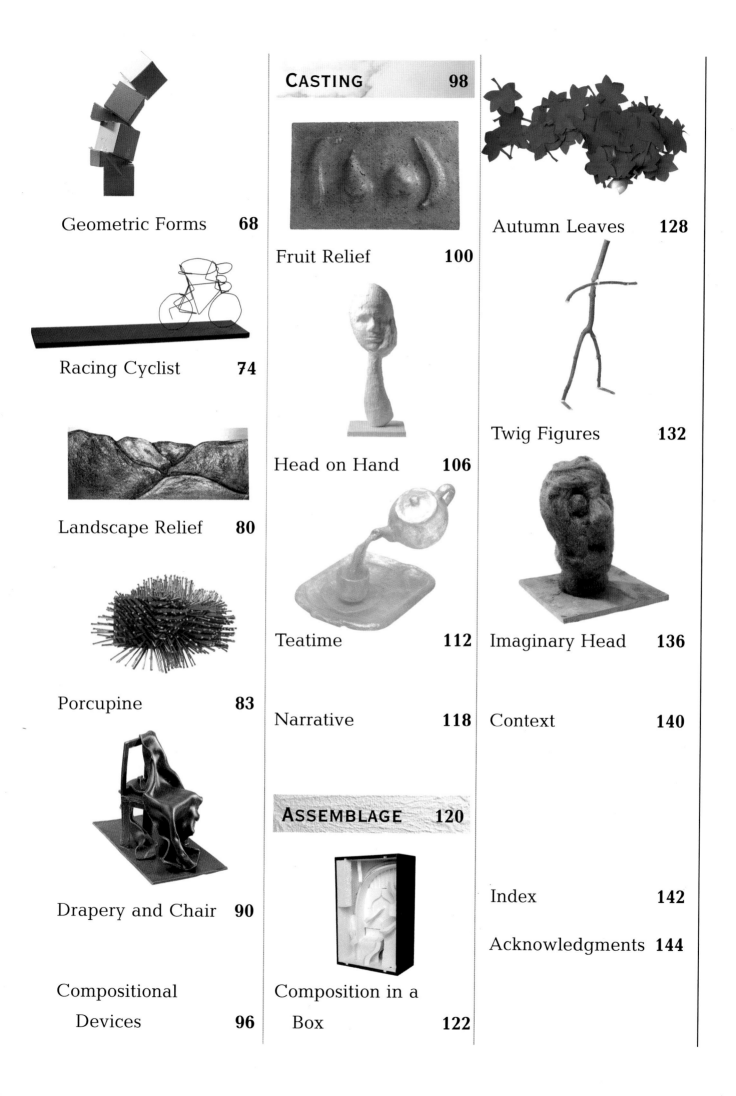

INTRODUCTION

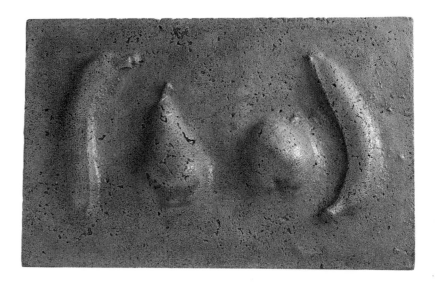

I N OUR DAY-TO-DAY lives we are surrounded by three-dimensional objects. With that familiarity in mind, there should be no reason why making sculpture – a three-dimensional object – should seem such a daunting task. However, as my experience of teaching sculpture has proved, it does. But, believe me, nothing could be further from the truth. I see students produce very credible sculptural statements within a very short space of time, some of whom have had no experience of making sculpture at all, and they really enjoy making them. You will be able to do the same.

▲ Rough and Smooth
pages 24–7

THE PROJECTS

THE PROJECTS IN this book have been designed with the newcomer to sculpture in mind. They do not need a lot of space and can be carried out in the home: on the kitchen table, in the garage or garden. No specialist equipment is needed and most of the tools required are those to be found in the average household tool box. Each project will introduce a different material to work with, some of which you will need to obtain from a specialist art material supplier, while others are more readily available. You will find more information in the equipment and materials sections on pages 10–13.

▲ Fruit Relief
pages 100–5

EXPLORING YOUR CREATIVITY

BY COMPLETING THE projects you will gain experience of five ways of making a sculpture: carving, modelling, construction, casting

and assemblage. But more importantly, the projects are an introduction to aspects of sculpture which apply to the whole range of sculpture-making techniques and which are extremely important to know and to understand. Gaining this knowledge and understanding will enable you to engage fully in the activity of making sculpture as the means to explore your own creativity. This is why the same aspect is dealt with in more than one project.

ASPECTS OF SCULPTURE

OF PARAMOUNT IMPORTANCE is a sculpture's relationship to gravity, which will affect its stability. This becomes immediately apparent when you do the "Architectural Tower" (see pp. 64–7). This leads on to the importance and use of the armature in sculpture; "Abstract Sculpture" (see pp. 32–5), "Swimming Dolphin" (see pp. 36–41) and "Mud and Straw Dog" (see pp. 54–9) serve to illustrate this point. But not every sculpture needs an armature and "Acrobats" (see pp. 42–7), "Seated Figure" (see pp. 48–53), "Drapery and Chair" (see pp. 90–5) and "Imaginary Head" (see pp. 136–9) investigate the limitations of the structural qualities of a variety of materials.

"Tactile Sculpture" (see pp. 18–23) and "Rough and Smooth" (see pp. 24–7) show how the surface of a sculpture describes its form. A variety of ways in which a base can be used are demonstrated in "Racing Cyclist" (see pp. 74–9), "Head on Hand" (see pp. 106–11) and "Teatime" (see pp. 112–17), while "Geometric Forms" (see pp. 68–73), "Composition in a Box" (see pp. 122–7) and "Autumn Leaves" (see pp. 128–31) deal with the differing functions of colour in sculpture. Two ways to make a relief sculpture are shown in "Landscape Relief" (see pp. 80–2) and "Fruit Relief" (see pp. 100–5); and the focus is on the use of a hand-held and a power tool in "Porcupine" (see pp. 83–9). In "Twig Figures" (see pp. 132–5) a sculpture is made with the minimum of manipulation of the material. The introductory text to each project gives a more extensive background to the points made above.

THE LANGUAGE OF SCULPTURE

WHETHER YOU INTEND to pursue sculpture as a leisure activity or to study sculpture in an educational institution, the projects in this book will provide a thorough grounding in the essentials that go towards understanding the language of sculpture. If you make sculptures that are within your own needs and aspirations you will gain immense satisfaction from this most potent of art forms.

9

▼ Racing cyclist
pages 74–9

EQUIPMENT

All the items on these pages have been used in the projects in this book. The tools listed below will be in most household tool boxes.

square
saw
surform
tape measure
wire brush
filling knife
pliers
electric drill
3 mm (⅛ in) drill bit
glue gun and glue sticks
hammer
G-clamp
secateurs
sandpaper
paintbrush
pencil
ruler
scissors
food mixer
old kitchen knife
rolling pin
saucepan
camping gas stove
sheet of glass
sponge
rags

The tools shown may already be in your tool box, but others may have to be obtained to complete some of the projects.

Small wire brush
With the original purpose of cleaning suede shoes, it is extremely useful for shaping fine details of expanded polystyrene.

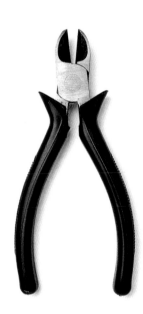

Wire cutters
With the specific purpose of cutting wire, this is a useful tool for cutting wire coathangers, chicken wire and binding wire.

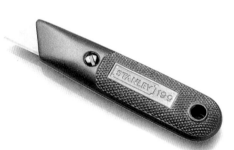

Craft knife
An essential piece of equipment which is useful for a variety of purposes. There is a large and small version, both of which have extremely sharp blades.

Zip bit
This comes in a variety of sizes and fits into an electric drill to enable you to drill a wide diameter hole.

Bradawl
A tool used to mark holes in wood prior to drilling. It is also extremely effective in making holes through thinner material, such as card.

Palette knife

Although really part of a painter's kit, it is useful for applying decorating filler to small areas of a sculpture's surface. Available from an art shop.

Tenon saw

Smaller than a general purpose saw, it is effective when you need to cut small pieces of wood or need to make specific angular cuts in wood.

Modelling tool

Made in either plastic or wood, they come in a variety of shapes and sizes and are used to apply and define a modelling material such as clay when making sculpture. Available from an art shop.

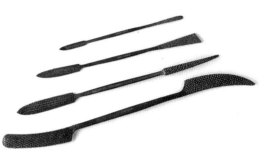

Rifflers

These are very small rasps used to smooth and shape small areas of a sculpture. They can be used on wood, stone, plaster or car body filler, and come in a variety of shapes.

Health and Safety

The items shown are for your own health and safety and so it is particularly important that you make use of them when recommended to do so in a project.

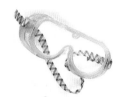

Dust/respirator mask

Use whenever a lot of dust is produced, such as when carving an aerated concrete block. It must also be used when using spray paints.

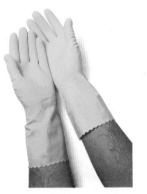

Rubber/canvas gloves

Wear them to protect your hands from sharp materials, such as chicken wire; and the irritants contained in certain materials, such as car body filler and cement. They also keep your hands clean.

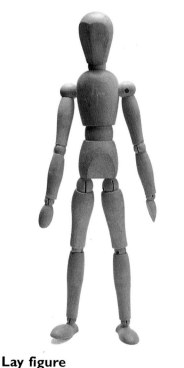

Clear goggles

Wear them whenever there is a danger of debris getting into your eye, such as when carving.

Barrier cream

Always rub some of this onto your hands before they come into contact with any material, particularly if you have sensitive skin.

Lay figure

An essential item for an artist interested in the human form. It provides a constant reference to the basic proportions of the figure. Available from an art shop.

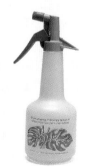

Water spray

Useful for keeping dust levels down when carving.

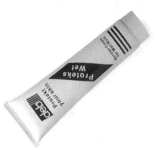

MATERIALS

The materials listed below are used for the projects and are likely to be found around the home or in the garage. If not, they are readily available from shops and inexpensive to buy.

The materials shown on these pages are less likely to be immediately to hand; you will need to obtain them for some of the projects.

PVA glue
wallpaper paste
decorating filler
car body filler
wire coathangers
binding wire
masking tape
clear adhesive tape
double-sided clear
adhesive tape
vegetable oil
washing-up liquid
clingfilm
aluminium foil
wire wool
blue, yellow, black, white,
red oxide spray paints
gold enamel paint
matt black paint
red emulsion paint
white eggshell paint
white spirit
3.5 cm (1½ in), 7.5 cm (3 in)
oval nails
2 cm (¾ in) panel pins
netting staples
hanging hooks

5 kg (11 lb) pack
ready-mixed sand and
cement
apple, pear, two bananas
various pieces of wood
MDF board
45 cm (18 in) dowelling
teapot, cup, saucer, tray
newspapers
card
found object
wooden drawer/box
wood offcuts
empty drink cans
twigs/small branches

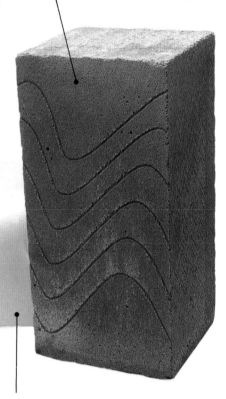

Aerated concrete block
Used in the construction of buildings, it is an extremely lightweight material and can be cut with a saw and shaped easily with a surform. Available from a builders' merchant.

Expanded polystyrene block
This material is extremely easy to shape with a wire brush, and provides a strong foundation for the addition of decorating filler. It is used as packing for large domestic items such as a fridge, and so should not prove difficult to obtain. It can also be bought from a specialist supplier.

Casting wax

A hard and brittle wax which when melted in a saucepan can be poured into a mould and left to cool to make a hard wax positive. Available from a specialist art material supplier.

Self-hardening clay

This synthetic clay handles exactly the same as standard clay, but when it is exposed to air it dries to a hard finish. Available from a general art and craft shop.

Modelling wax

When cool it is relatively hard; but when warmed by kneading in the hands it becomes very soft and pliable. It has a similar consistency to clay and can be modelled in the same way. Available from a specialist art material supplier.

Polystyrene tiles

With the same qualities as the polystyrene block, they are more suited for use in a relief sculpture than one in the round. Available from a DIY shop.

Chicken wire

A flexible wire mesh sheet that is easy to cut. It is useful for laying over an armature to develop a sculpture's form and for reinforcement when making a cast sculpture. Available from a DIY shop or garden centre.

Art straws

Usually made of paper, they are useful only for making temporary sculptures. Available from either a general art and craft shop or a children's toy shop.

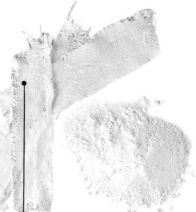

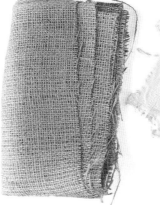

Plaster-impregnated bandage

A combination of thin mesh bandage and plaster which, once soaked in water, will set hard very quickly. It is most suitable for producing thin casts, particularly direct casts taken from the figure. Available from a specialist art material shop.

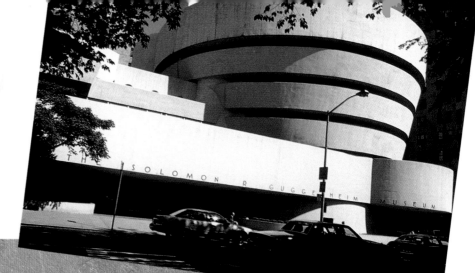

GETTING STARTED

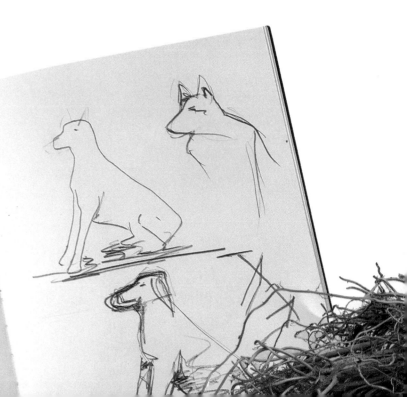

▲ Cut interesting photographs from magazines and newspapers and stick them in a sketchbook or loose folder.

Ostensibly, making sculpture is the manipulation of a material to give it form. "But what form shall I give it?" I hear you ask. This is a very good question, but it's not one that I can answer. What I can do, though, is to point out various avenues to explore which will enable you to come up with your own personal answer. After all, as you develop your sculpture-making skills you will also want your sculpture to express your own creative thoughts and interests.

AN INFORMATION RESOURCE

Having a collection of source material can help you to start a sculpture. Try to be more aware of your surroundings and their sculptural possibilities and, at the same time, develop the habit of keeping a sketchbook and having it with you wherever you go. Look upon it as a visual diary, not as a repository of major works of art.

Use your sketchbook to make drawings, to note that flash of inspiration that came to you while sitting on the bus, or record the interesting form of the fallen tree trunk you saw while walking through the park. Make drawings of anything and everything that

▼ Always carry a sketchbook to record anything and everything that interests you.

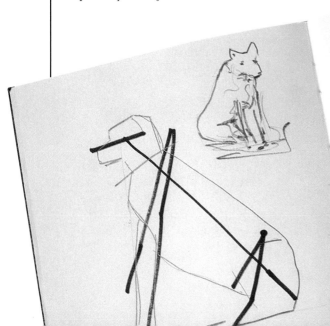

▼ Keep an eye open for unusual shapes that might be incorporated into a sculpture.

interests you; a drawing could be a quick notation to record a particular moment in time. Constant drawing will help you gain a greater understanding of form, especially human form, and naturally occurring forms. You will find these to be a continuing source of inspiration for making sculpture. However you make a drawing, it is something that you will be able to refer to at a later date.

Your sketchbook can also be used to store interesting photographs cut from newspapers or magazines, or photocopied from books. You do not need to have a specific use in mind when you cut them out; the important thing is that you have made the selection because, as with the drawings, they can be referred to at a later date when they could be applicable to a sculpture you are planning.

Surface and texture in sculpture are both very important. Building up a collection of objects with interesting surfaces, textures or shapes will prove useful when you make drawings towards a piece of sculpture. You will find that the most unlikely item can become an important source of information for a piece of sculpture.

MAKING SCULPTURE DIRECTLY

OF COURSE, NOT ALL sculpture depends on preplanning or the use of specific references. For instance, a sculpture could be made by employing a specific process or technique, and this process or technique determines the form of the sculpture, such as the repetition of the same shape. The form of a

▼ Be aware of the texture of objects around you.

sculpture could be determined by the material it is made from, for instance the form of a carving could be derived from the eccentric shapes contained in a block.

Other sculptures are also an invaluable resource for providing inspiration for your own sculptures. It is certainly worth familiarizing yourself with sculptures past and present because you, after all, are its future.

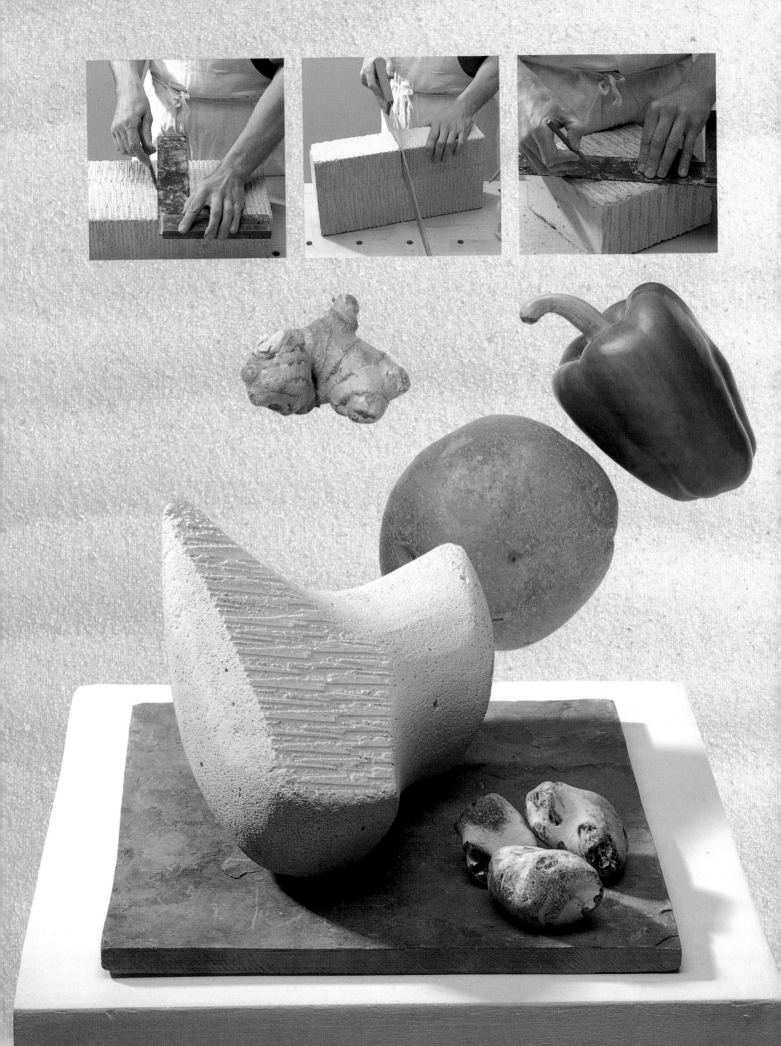

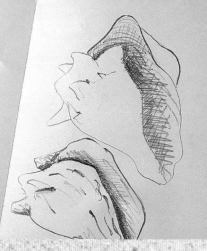

CARVING

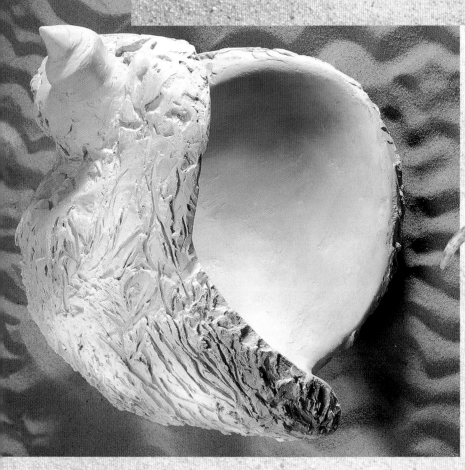

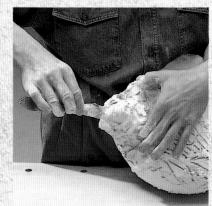

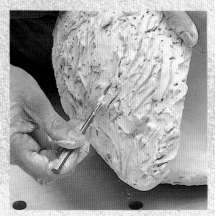

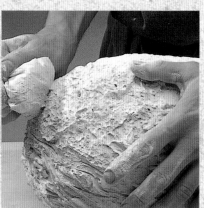

TACTILE SCULPTURE

C ARVING IS ONE of the basic sculpting techniques whereby a solid block of material is cut and shaped into the desired form. Here, you will be making a hand-held sculpture – intended for the blind – to be understood in a tactile rather than a visual way.

Sculpture makes a strong appeal to our sense of touch. You may notice that some sculptures in museums or public galleries – usually made of bronze or stone – have a part which is especially shiny. This is where the sculpture has been touched and stroked by visitors over the years. Today we are invariably discouraged from touching sculpture, which is a shame for, by exploring the surface of a piece with your hands, you are able to respond to its tactile quality: *ie* is it rough or smooth? Is it pleasant to touch or does it send a shiver of revulsion down your spine?

The material that you are going to carve is an aerated concrete block; a very soft material, easy to saw and shape with a surform. Because this sculpture is intended to be "seen" with the hands, they will have an important part to play in its development. Use them to continually explore its surface at all stages during its making. Don't forget that a successful sculptured surface is one that allows the hand to travel freely around it, moving easily from one worked area to another.

▲ To develop your sense of touch, get a friend to put an object in a bag. Close your eyes, slip your hands in the bag and attempt to identify the mystery "thing" just by touch.

▲ Use your hands to explore objects with textured or unusual surfaces – fruit, vegetables, household items. Nothing could make clearer the importance of the surface in describing form.

Materials
aerated concrete block

Equipment
**tape measure
pencil
square and ruler
saw
surform
sandpaper**

Health/Safety
**dust mask
clear goggles
apron
water spray**

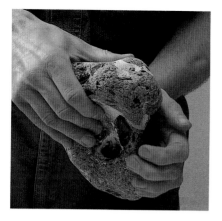

1 Start by using your hands as your eyes to feel around objects, such as this rock. This will enable you to understand how a surface describes the form of an object. The simpler a form is, the easier it is for your hands to move around the surface.

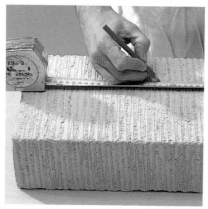

2 The aerated concrete block will need to be sawn in half, as it is too large for a hand-held sculpture. Use a tape measure to mark the halfway point on the block.

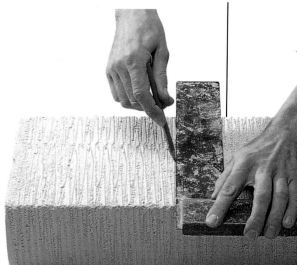

3 From this mark use a square to draw a vertical line on the large face of the block. From this line use the square to mark another line at right angles to it on one of the long, thin sides.

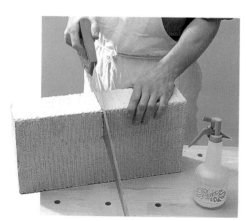

4 Begin sawing the block in two. You will find that the saw will cut through the block very easily. There will be a lot of dust, so make sure that you are wearing a dust mask, clear goggles and an apron while working on the block. Also keep a water spray handy to keep down the dust levels in the air.

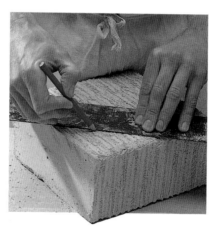

5 With your tape measure, mark the midpoint along the top edge of the block and do the same along an adjacent edge. Use the ruler to draw a line joining these midpoints, then, using the square, continue the line at right angles to the top face on both adjacent thin side faces.

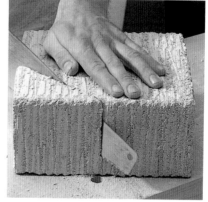

6 Saw off the marked corner wedge and discard it. Hold the block firm and steady as you are sawing.

Safety

- **Wear a dust mask and clear goggles**
- **Have a water spray to hand to keep the dust level down**

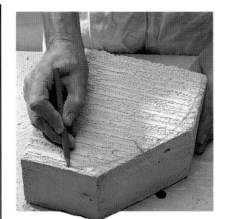
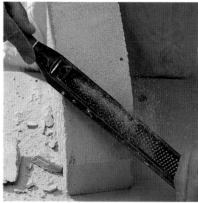
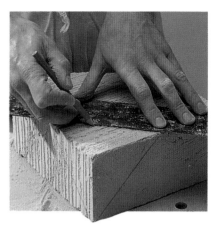

7 Lie the block down on the table. Measure and mark the midpoint of the diagonal edge. Draw an even curved line from the far corner of the block to the opposite corner. The apex of the curved line should touch the midpoint mark on the diagonal edge.

8 With the surform, round off this face of the block using the curved line you have drawn as your guide.

9 Place the block face-down on the bench. Measure and mark the midpoints of the top two remaining straight edges. From the bottom corner of the block draw a diagonal line to this mark on both of the thin side faces. Then draw a line on the face of the block joining the two midpoint marks.

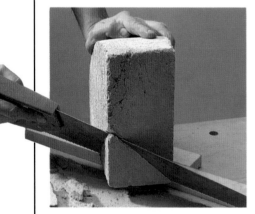

10 Place the block on timber so that it is raised above the surface of the bench. Holding the block steady, saw a diagonal cut along the lines marked on the block.

11 You have now reached ▷ the stage when the block is losing its geometric shape and is becoming tactile. With the surform you can now start to feel your way around the block.

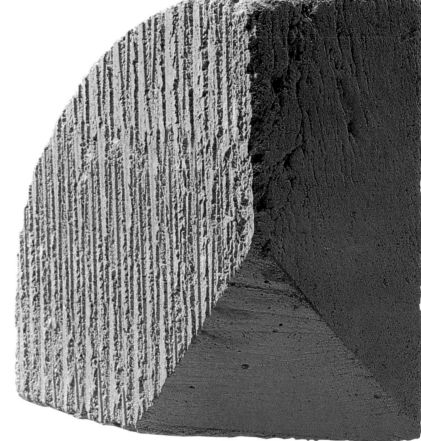

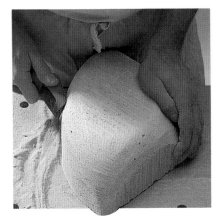

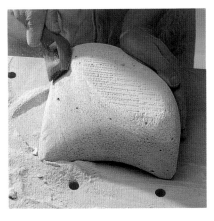

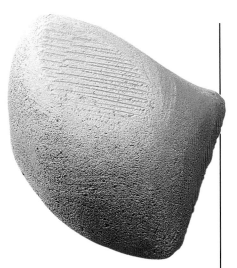

12 Use the surform to smooth down the geometric shape of the block further. From now on make sure that your hand is in close contact with the surface of the block. You will then be able to know how to develop the form of the sculpture as you shape the surface.

13 Use your surform to smooth away the corner of the block. When using this tool imagine that it is your hand – this will help you feel your way over the surface of the block.

14 With the block lying flat on the bench, you can see that the surface is beginning to curve away underneath it. Use your hands to follow this surface around to the other side. Now turn the block over and start to work this side with your tool.

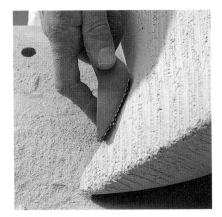

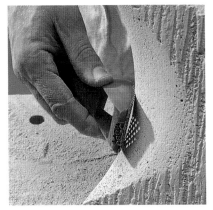

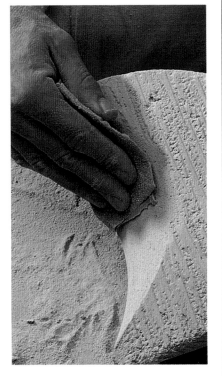

15 Hold the block securely in one hand. With the other start to shape the flat side. As before, use the surform as an extension of your hand to deepen and smooth away the developing concave surface.

16 This picture shows how *not* to use the surform. Do *not* hold the tool at right angles to the surface. Keep the blade flat and parallel to the surface of the block. Be aware that the shape of your tool will determine the final form of the sculpture.

17 Alternate using the surform with sandpaper. This helps to shape and develop more intricate parts of the surface, as well as bringing your hand into closer contact with the surface of the sculpture as you shape it.

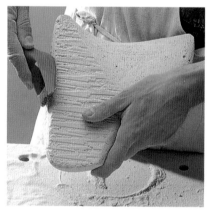

18 The concave shape is now fully developed on the other side of the block. Note how its form is related to the shape of the tool blade. One area of the original block has been left unworked; it provides a contrast between a rough surface and the smoother curve of the main part.

19 The block is now truly appealing to the hands. Use the surform to develop a concave surface on top of the sculpture, making sure that you keep the blade flush with the surface you are shaping.

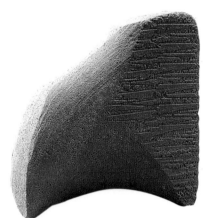

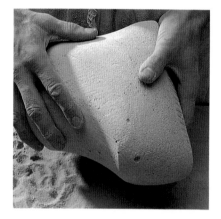

20 The completed concave surface on top causes the surfaces to flow into one another, allowing easy movement of the hands around the piece, with no distinctions between front, back or sides.

21 When the block reaches this stage it is extremely important to use your hands to feel your way around the sculpture. They must understand the form, and so make decisions regarding further shaping.

22 After investigating the sculpture with your hands, smooth away the straight edges of the original block slightly.

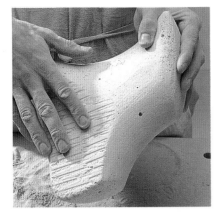

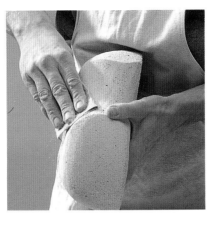

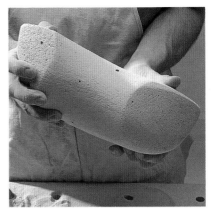

23 Keep feeling your way around the sculpture, paying particular attention to the rough surface to ensure an adequate transition from the rough to the smooth.

24 A smoothing down with sandpaper will help to further define and refine the form of the sculpture.

25 Finally, "test" the sculpture with your hands, keeping your eyes closed. This will reveal any inconsistencies in the surface as your hands move around the sculpture. You will discover which areas need to be smoothed down further or perhaps reshaped.

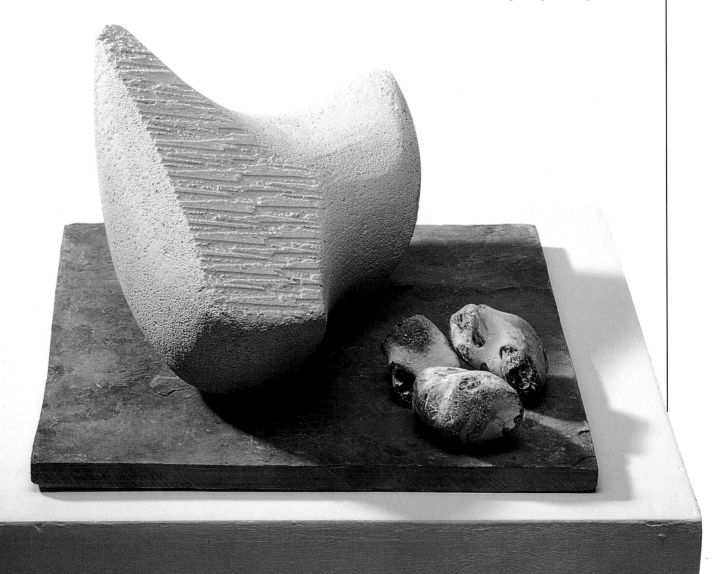

ROUGH AND SMOOTH

T HIS PROJECT INVOLVES two sculptural techniques – carving and modelling. First, you carve a block of expanded polystyrene – but, once shaped, that is not the end of the story. Instead, a surface of decorating filler is added on top, using a technique known as direct modelling. You then shape the decorating filler to create a variety of different surface textures.

Intrinsic to this project is an appreciation of the contrasting natures of these techniques: *ie* carving is a reductive and modelling an additive process. Having an understanding of these two techniques will help you to decide on the type of sculpture you wish to pursue in the future.

It is important to point out that this project is not just a case of *creating* different surface textures. An initial period of thought needs to go into how to develop them. Here, the inspiration comes from the natural world with its vast assortment of forms, surfaces and textures. Remember, you are not attempting to replicate the conch in every detail, but rather to search for the essence of the shell in both its form and texture.

You will find that the expanded polystyrene is extremely easy to shape with a wire brush. It creates a good deal of mess, so make sure that you do this project in a suitable area.

You can carve packing polystyrene used to protect consumer household goods; it is invariably discarded by shops or households when large items are delivered. If you have none on hand there are companies that sell it. The decorating filler used in the modelling is available from DIY shops. Easily mixed, it does not set quickly so you have time to apply it and work it into the appearance you want. When set, however, it is extremely hard.

▲ A conch shell is highly sculptural; and its rounded shape is well suited to the carving and shaping of a polystyrene block.

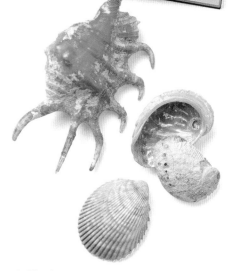

▲ The interplay between the rough outer and smooth inner surfaces provides textural interest. Explore these facets in a series of drawings before you start carving.

Materials

**expanded polystyrene block
– 28 × 28 × 19 cm
(11 × 11 × 7½ in)
decorating filler**

Equipment

**sketchbook
pencil
felt pen
saw
wire brush
plastic container
filling knife
sandpaper
large nail
polythene bag
surform
riffler**

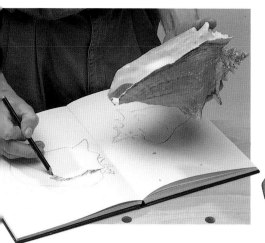

1 Make a series of drawings investigating the interior and exterior aspects of the shell, paying particular attention to its spiral form and interior. Bear in mind that you must relate this form to the block of polystyrene.

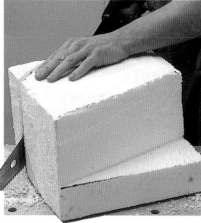

2 Mark out and saw off a wedge 28 cm (11 in) long, 13 cm (5 in) high and 10 cm (4 in) at its widest point from the front face of the block. Mark 7.5 cm (3 in) in from the corner on two adjacent top edges, draw a line at right angles to the corner from one to the other and saw off this corner of the block.

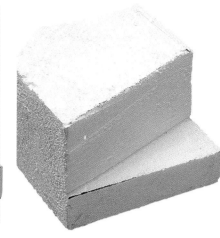

3 Dispose of all the waste material cut from the block. It now has its basic shape, enabling you to carve a form containing an interior space.

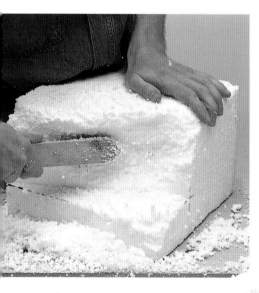

4 Use the wire brush to carve into the block. Eliminate as much polystyrene as possible to create the interior space. Continue working your way around the polystyrene to create a rounded form.

5 Because of the ease with which the polystyrene can be shaped, it does not take long to lose the geometry of the original block. The interior space is enclosed by a rounded, shell-like form. ▼

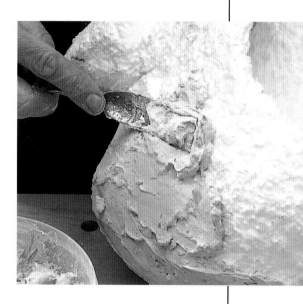

6 Add water to the decorating filler and mix until it has the consistency of cream cheese. Use a filling knife to apply a layer approximately 3 mm (⅛ in) thick over the surface.

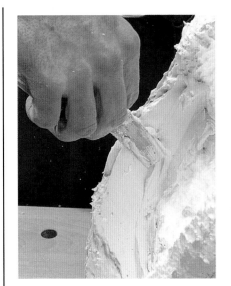

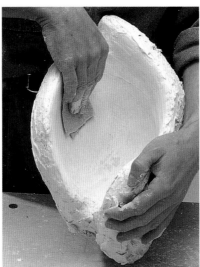

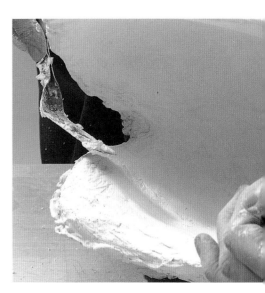

7 Cover the whole of the surface of the polystyrene, including the interior. Try as much as possible to keep the filler to a smooth level, especially in the interior surface. Once covered, leave the filler to dry for 2 or 3 hours.

8 When the filler is dry, smooth down the interior as much as possible with sandpaper, removing the high points of filler.

9 Apply another coat of decorating filler to the interior surface. Concentrate on filling up any holes and gaps in the surface. Leave it to dry and then once again use sandpaper to smooth it down to create a smooth surface.

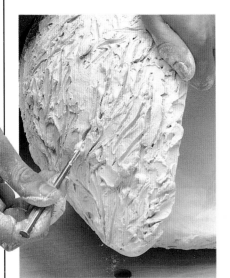

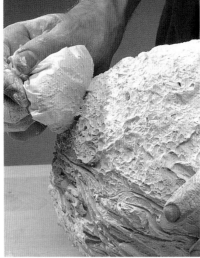

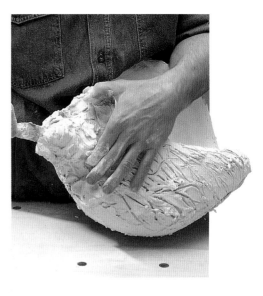

10 Apply a second thick coat of filler to the top of the sculpture and, while it is still wet, drag a nail through it to create a wavy line effect.

11 On the underside of the sculpture, add filler and, with a rolled up polythene bag, push this into the surface of the filler and then quickly lift it off to create this stippled effect.

12 On the pointed end of the sculpture, build up a really thick area of filler. Let this dry, then add more filler, building up a thick mass. Turn your filling knife round and pull it out to build up a spiral effect.

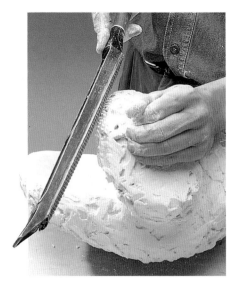 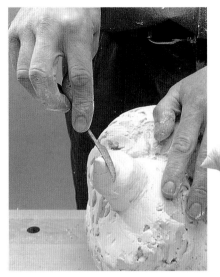 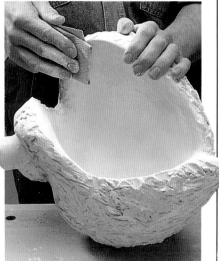

13 Once the large masses of filler are dry, use a surform to shape the spiral. Notice what an interesting texture is created by the surform levelling off across high points of filler.

14 Use a riffler to further refine and shape the spiral form, finishing off in a point.

15 Use sandpaper to give the spiral form its final definition. Continue to sand the interior space, paying special attention to sharpening the edge between the rough and smooth surfaces.

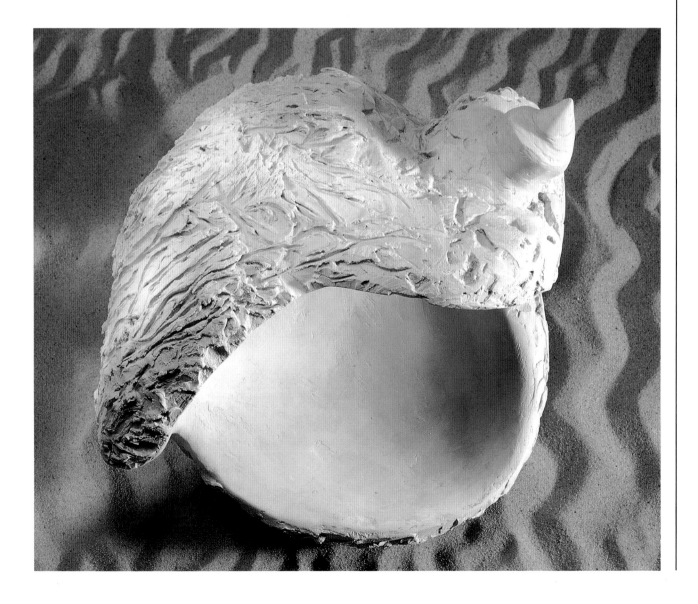

SURFACE

THE FORM OF A SCULPTURE is described by its surface which encourages the eye to move around the sculpture. The way a surface is defined determines how well the viewer can make sense of a sculpture's form. In this respect naturally occurring forms are an important source of reference and can provide inspiration.

The surface of a sculpture with solid forms is especially important as it describes the mass and volume and consequently the way the forms articulate against one another. A successful sculpture does not require a smooth surface; but sometimes a smooth surface provides the best resolution for a sculpture to be understood and appreciated, especially when the form is large or simple.

A variety of surface textures can be used as a compositional device to enhance and define the forms within the sculpture, especially when carving forms of different size and shape from a single block.

The surface, therefore, is of primary importance in enabling the viewer to make sense of a sculpture's form. The sculptures in this section illustrate how careful control of the surface has been put to good effect.

▲ **Chris Dunseath**
OFFERING

Each of the elements carved from this block of Portland stone has been emphasized by alternating smooth and rough surfaces. The sculpture was influenced by the ritual offering tables from Egyptian and Indian cultures.
50 × 45 × 39 cm
(20¾ × 18¾ × 15¼ in)

▼ **Antony Denning**
MOEBIUS STONE

This carving in French limestone has one smooth continuous surface running right round the sculpture, an antidote to the six surfaces of the block from which it was carved. The sculpture was inspired by "The Moebius Band", a twisted strip having one continuous surface and one continuous edge.
300 mm (11¾ in) long

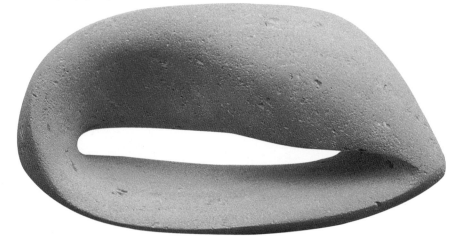

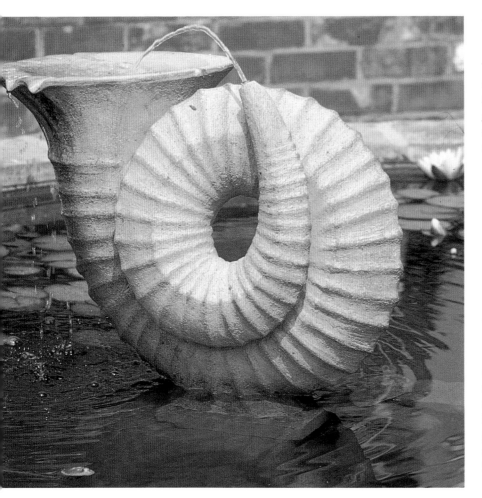

Althea Wynne
AMMONITE FOUNTAIN

This functional sculpture made from coiled stoneware clay uses well the form of an ammonite fossil. Great attention has been given to recreating the surface of the fossil on the clay.
60 cm (23½ in) high

Peter Randall-Page
STILL LIFE

A large three-piece sculpture directly carved in Kilkenny limestone, sited in the open air. The forms of the sculpture are based on three threatened species: the pupa of the Swallowtail butterfly, the shell of a land snail and the fruit of the Spindle tree.
138.5 cm (54½ in) tallest element

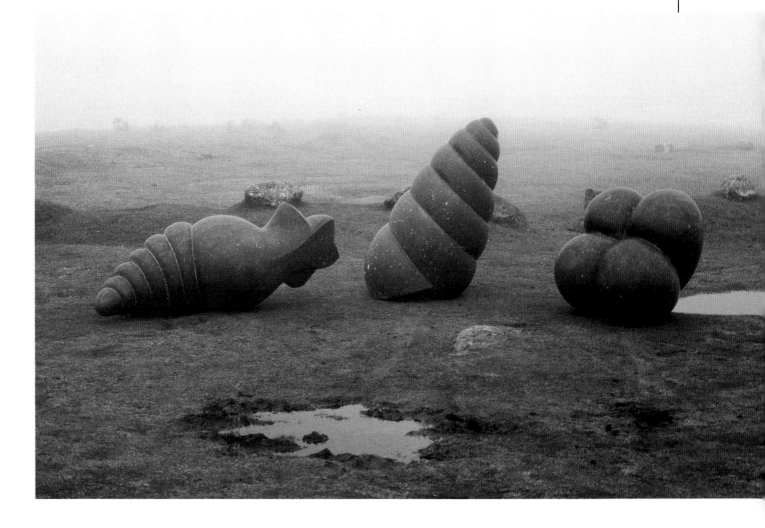

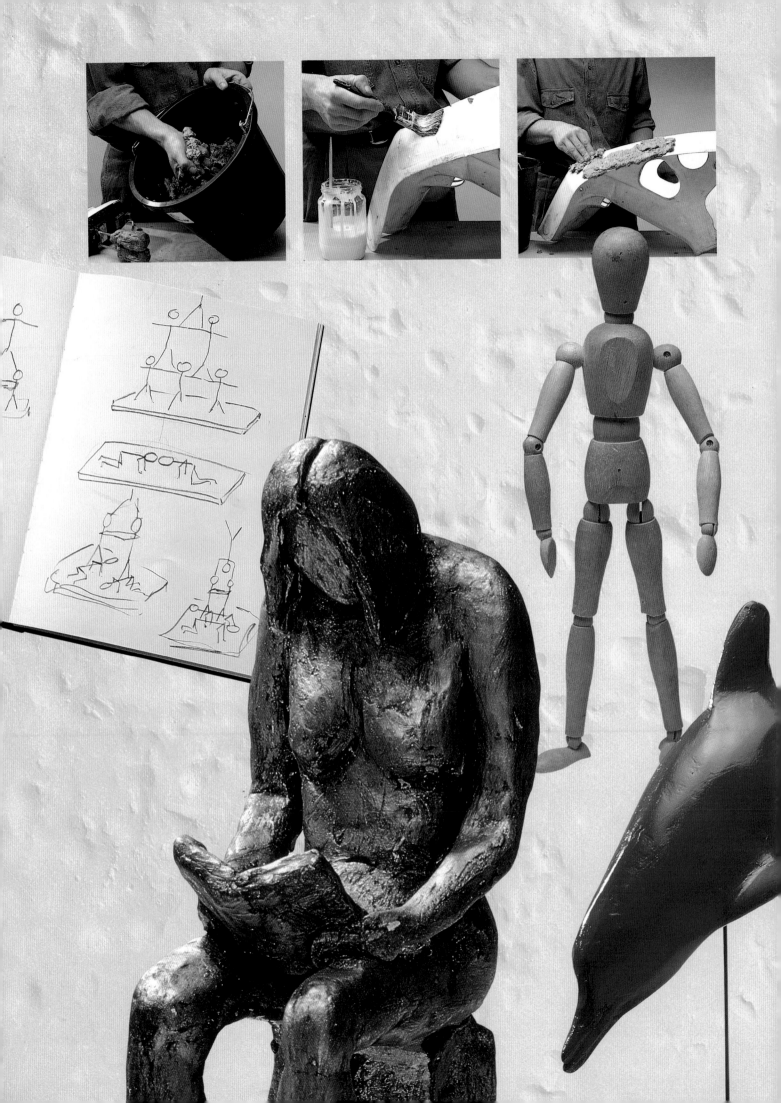

2

MODELLING

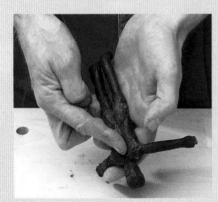
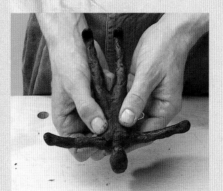

ABSTRACT
SCULPTURE

SOMETIMES THE MATERIAL you want to use in a proposed sculpture is unable to support itself – a large work in clay for example. In such a situation, the armature – a rigid structure – comes into its own. Similar to the skeleton inside our bodies, the armature both supports and gives shape to the medium which surrounds it.

An armature can be used as a temporary support for the modelled sculpture until it is cast in another more durable material. Alternatively, when a harder, more resilient material has been chosen – as in "Swimming Dolphin" (see pp. 36–41) – it will stay inside the finished sculpture as an important structural element of it. In either case, it is important to appreciate that an armature will largely dictate the shape of the piece. This is only logical, because to be effective in its supportive role it needs to be as close as possible to the exposed surface of the modelling medium. You will be unable to pile up and model your clay because it will fall off. This simple fact means that you are unable to drastically alter the form of the sculpture from that of its underlying armature. So, before designing an armature, make sure that it will provide an underpinning that adequately reflects your original concept.

In this project you will be modelling material directly onto an armature, without the necessity of having a specific design or concept in mind. The success of this approach depends on finding an interesting discarded object. Remember that the final sculpture will be more visually interesting if the viewer is unable to identify the "found" object but instead gains enjoyment from its form.

Here papier mâché is used as the modelling material. It has a soft and plastic consistency in its pulp form, and is used in a similar way to clay. It dries to an extremely hard finish, which can be sealed with PVA glue or painted.

▲
▼ Look for interestingly-shaped objects in your garage, garden shed and attic. Extend your search to builders' skips and refuse tips.

Materials

found object
wallpaper paste
newspapers
PVA glue (diluted)
paint

Equipment

bucket
scissors
food mixer
paintbrush

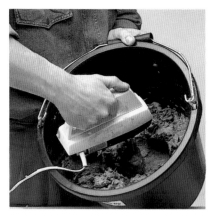

1 This interesting object was found in the refuse from a motorcycle repair shop. In fact it is the fairing from a small motorcycle. Placed in this position you can appreciate its interesting sculptural possibilities.

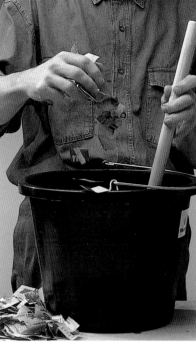

3 After several hours of soaking, the paper begins to break up, forming a pulp. Use a food mixer to speed this process up.

2 In a bucket make a mix of wallpaper paste. To this mix add strips of newspaper which have been cut with scissors to approx 7.5 × 5 cm (3 × 2 in). Stir the newspaper well in and let the mixture soak for 24 hours.

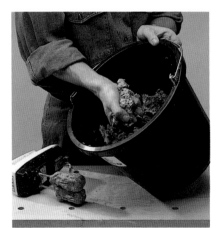

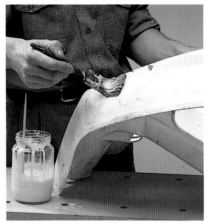

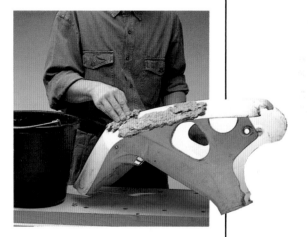

4 After mixing well, a thick paper pulp results. This can be worked in a similar way to clay.

5 Because papier mâché does not defy gravity it needs to be applied to the underside first. Turn the object over and paint on a generous coat of diluted PVA glue. Brush on a small area at a time.

6 Start adding small quantities of papier mâché, a little at a time, to the area treated with the PVA glue.

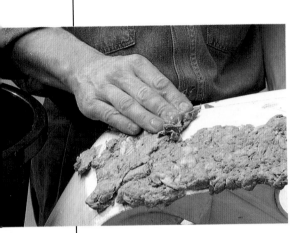

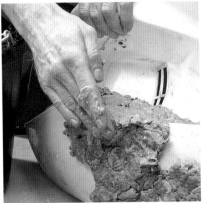

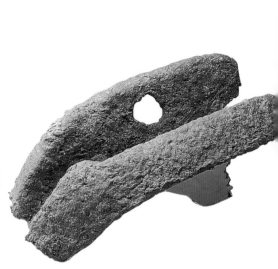

7 When you apply the papier mâché make sure that you press it firmly onto the surface of the object. Blend it into the adjacent paper mâché.

8 When modelling onto vertical surfaces, tip the object so that it becomes horizontal. This makes for easier modelling, and also lessens the chances of the papier mâché falling off while you are applying it.

9 The underside has now been completely covered with papier mâché. Note the interesting surface produced by the papier mâché, as well as the fact that the overall form of the sculpture truly reflects the armature underneath it. Leave the partially completed work to dry.

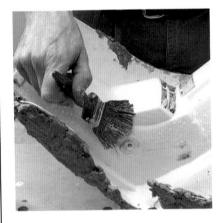

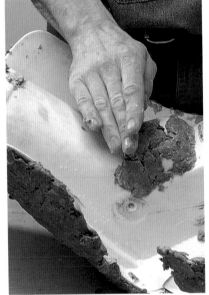

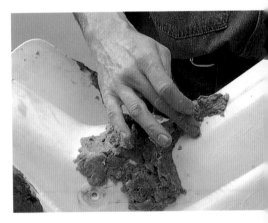

10 Turn the object back over and apply a generous coat of PVA glue to this side.

11 Model the papier mâché over the opening on the central spine, patting it firmly down.

12 This area has small and particular detailing, so apply the papier mâché in small amounts to allow this detail to stand out.

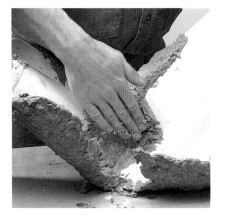

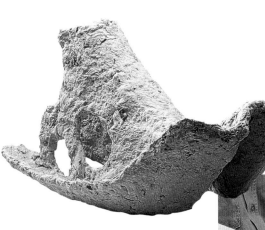

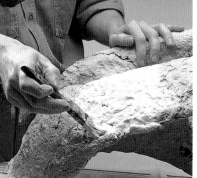

13 Since one side of the object was broken, this opening is left as part of the final sculpture. Model the papier mâché so it closely follows the profile of the broken plastic.

14 The sculpture is now finished. Allow the piece to dry out. The result is a very lightweight sculpture with a hard and textured surface.

15 Apply two coats of diluted ▷ PVA glue, allowing the first coat to dry before adding another. This will seal the surface. Then paint the underside of the sculpture. When this is dry, turn the sculpture over and paint the upper part with a contrasting or complementary colour.

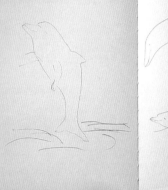

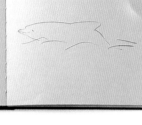

From the photographs make some drawings in your sketchbook. Use only line drawing to record the profiles of dolphins; this will help you decide the shape of the wire armature.

SWIMMING DOLPHIN

A S DEMONSTRATED IN "Abstract Sculpture" (see pp. 32–5) the shape of an armature will always be instrumental in defining the final form of the sculpture. In this project, the object is to design and *make* an armature which does just that, at the same time remembering that you must provide a stable foundation for the modelling material. The project will help you appreciate the importance of precise planning, of ensuring that the armature is sturdily made and that the chosen subject is one whose form can be easily translated into an armature. The shape of a dolphin is ideal, primarily because its straightforward outline is one which is easily adapted to a wire armature. I decided to portray a dolphin caught mid-flight, jumping out of the water.

The second aim of the project is to produce a base, both to sustain the feeling of a captured moment of time, and to act as a support. It should be as unobtrusive as possible, holding the sculpture in such a way that the viewer is aware only of the dolphin.

Wire coathangers will provide the support and, together with newspaper and masking tape, describe the form of the armature and, consequently, the sculpture. Using the technique known as direct modelling, car body filler (available from car spare shops) is applied to the armature and built up to result in the final sculpture. Its quick-setting attributes allow it to be shaped and smoothed down to a very fine finish.

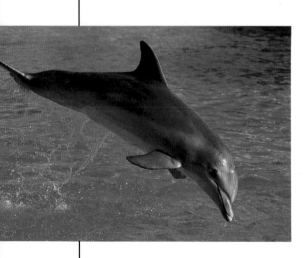

▲ Look in books and magazines for pictures of dolphins. Whether in or out of the water, their form invokes a sense of movement, a dynamic sculptural attribute.

Materials

wire coathangers
binding wire
paper or card
newspaper
masking tape
car body filler
decorating filler
MDF block 10 × 10 × 2 cm
(4 × 4 × ⅝ in)
grey spray paint

Equipment

felt-tip pen
pliers
scissors
filling knife
palette knife
modelling knife
riffler
sandpaper
electric drill
3 mm (⅛ in) drill bit
bradawl

Health/Safety

rubber gloves
respirator mask

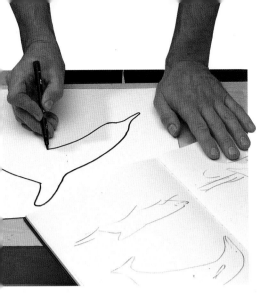

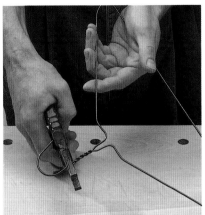

1 Use a felt-tip pen to draw the outline of a dolphin from the drawings in your sketchbook onto a piece of paper or card.

2 Use pliers to cut the hook off a wire coathanger.

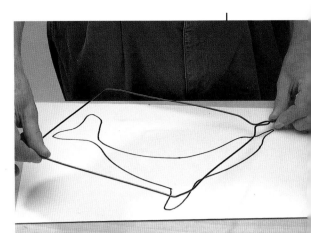

3 Position the coathanger over your drawing, holding the twisted end of the hanger over the dolphin's nose. Pull the hanger outwards, front and back.

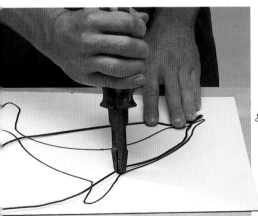

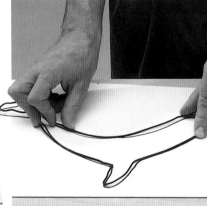

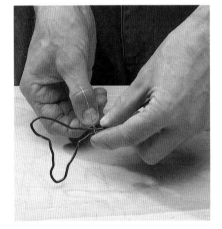

4 Continuing to hold the wire firmly over the drawn outline, use the pliers to bend the wire so that it follows the outline of the drawing as closely as possible.

5 Hold the head section firmly down on the drawing. Pinch together the tail section of the armature.

6 Wrap a short length of binding wire around the tail section. Twist the ends around once with your fingers, then use pliers to twist two more turns to tighten the wire.

Safety

- **Work in a well ventilated area when using car body filler or spray paint**
- **Wear rubber gloves and a respirator mask**
- **Make sure that all surrounding areas are covered with newspaper when using spray paint**

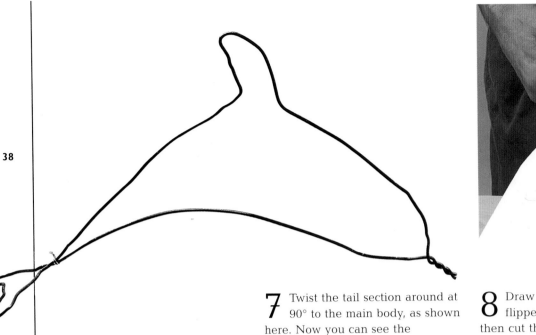

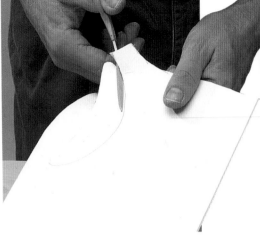

7 Twist the tail section around at 90° to the main body, as shown here. Now you can see the armature taking on the form of the dolphin.

8 Draw the outline of the flippers on a piece of card, then cut them out.

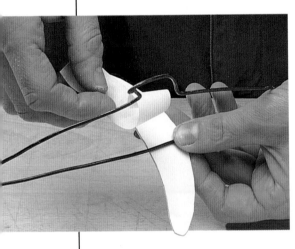

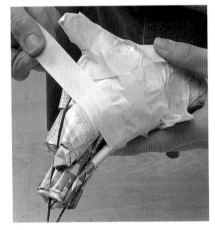

11 The newspapers and tape are used specifically to indicate the mass of a dolphin. Take care not to add too much of either. ▼

9 Tape the flippers onto the underside of the armature with masking tape.

10 Fill up the inside of the wire armature with newspaper. Hold it in place with masking tape, ensuring that you wind the tape around tightly.

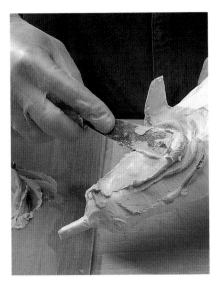

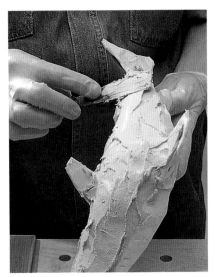

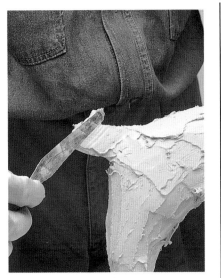

12 Mix only a small amount of car body filler at a time. Place equal lengths of filler and hardener on a piece of old board. Mix the two elements together to achieve an even colouring. Spread a thin layer over the surface of the armature.

13 When spreading the filler, follow the form of the armature. Avoid building up a thick layer which detracts from this form.

14 Using a palette knife, apply the filler to the fins and flippers.

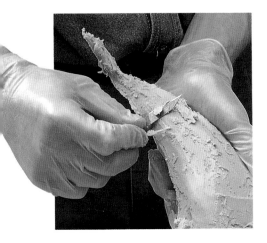

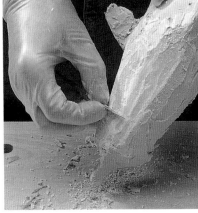

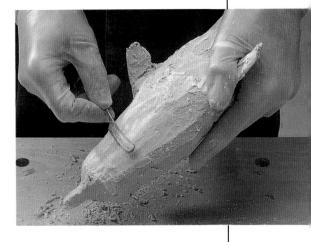

15 Just before the filler sets completely it takes on a cheese-like consistency. At this point, use a modelling knife to trim and cut back any excess filler, while at the same time developing the form of the dolphin.

16 As the filler gets harder, use the blade of your modelling knife to scrape the surface to further define the form of the dolphin.

17 When the filler has set, use a riffler to smooth and shape the surface of the sculpture.

18 Continue adding filler, cutting back with the modelling knife and shaping with the knife blade and riffler. Finally, rub with sandpaper to create a smooth finish.

19 After this initial sanding, fill in any small holes or uneven patches in the surface with decorating filler. When this dries, it can be sanded level with the car body filler.

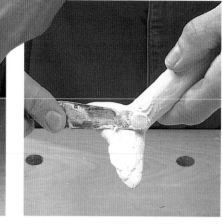

20 The finished dolphin has an extremely hard surface. Its mouth was shaped using the riffler. You can still see the areas where decorating filler was used.

23 Insert a 23 cm (9 in) length of coathanger wire into the base hole. Insert the other end of the wire into the hole on the underside of the dolphin. Since this hole is larger than the wire, you can position the dolphin so that it rests gracefully on the wire.

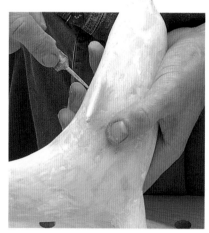

22 On the underside of the dolphin, between the flippers, make a hole with a bradawl. Twist the bradawl around until you break through the surface of the filler. Continue to turn the bradawl in a circular motion to increase the diameter of the hole.

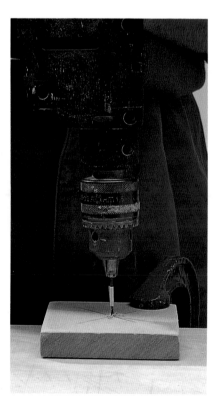

21 Clamp the wooden base to your work surface. Drill a 3 mm (⅛ in) hole into its centre.

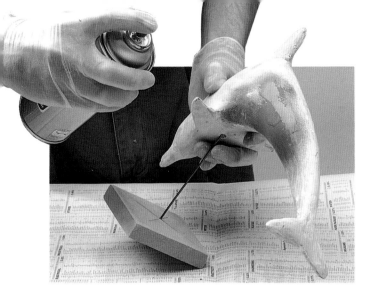

24 Wearing rubber gloves and a face mask, and with surrounding areas masked with newspaper, spray the dolphin and the stand with grey paint. When the paint is dry any uneven areas on the surface of the dolphin will show up clearly. Fill these and the hole around the support with decorating filler. Sand smooth when dry, then spray the whole sculpture again.

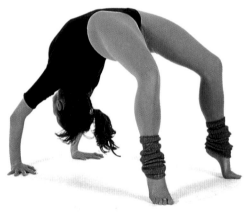

▼ Explore various groupings and positions of figures in your sketchbook. Detail is not important at this stage.

ACROBATS

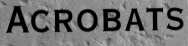

In "ABSTRACT SCULPTURE" (see pp. 32–5) emphasis was placed on the ability of an armature to support the modelling material, as well as on how the armature determines the final form of the sculpture. This project concentrates on producing a sculpture which does not rely on an armature; one in which the subject matter, combined with the structural limitations of the material, determines the final form.

You will be using modelling wax (readily available from an art materials shop). It comes in a block which looks hard and brittle, but it is easily cut with a knife, and requires only the heat from your hands to knead it into a soft, malleable modelling material. Left alone, it quickly cools and acquires an inherent strength. Another important property of modelling wax is its ability to retain the marks and impressions of the process by which it was formed. This can be highly useful when conveying expression and emotion. So, when modelling, never become too obsessed with obliterating or smoothing out such marks.

Using the human figure as the subject for this sculpture automatically gives it an identity, but you are not aiming for an accurate representation of a particular person or persons; instead you will be attempting to produce a generic figure in the correct proportions and placement of head, arms, torso and legs.

In order to determine the proportions of the figures, a wooden lay figure is used as the model. This is an extremely useful artists' tool; one to which you can constantly refer when making figurative drawings or sculptures. Take your measurements from the lay figure and reduce them by 50 percent to produce a scale plan of the figure on paper. Use the plan as a guide when making the wax figures, ensuring that each of the five remains proportionally correct.

◀ Once you have decided on the positioning of the group, look at pictures of gymnasts and acrobats in different positions and make some more detailed sketches.

Materials

modelling wax

Equipment

sketchbook
pencil
tape measure
ruler
lay figure
paper
old kitchen knife
clingfilm
modelling board
modelling knife

Health/Safety

barrier cream

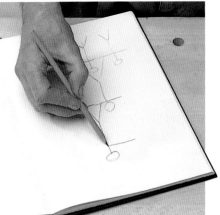

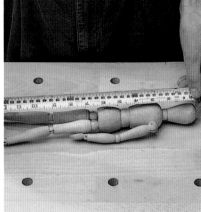

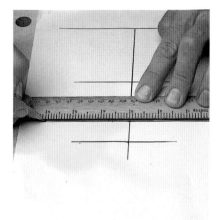

1 Make some drawings in your sketchbook, exploring various structural configurations of figures. Do not become distracted by particulars but concentrate on the sculptural possibilities.

2 Measure the length of the lay figure. This one is 30 cm (12 in) long; you can see that the head, at 5 cm (2 in) long, is a sixth of the overall height of the figure. This is a general rule of art, and one that is useful to learn, *ie* the ideal height of the human figure is six heads.

3 Reduce each of the measurements of the lay figure by 50 percent, then draw a simple plan of the wax figure. Here the reduced measurement of the outstretched arms is drawn onto the paper.

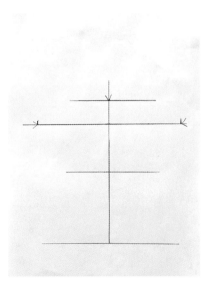

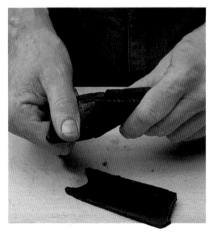

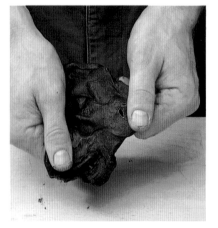

4 The 15 cm (6 in) point from the baseline is marked on the vertical by an arrow. A further 2.5 cm (1 in) above this point is allowed for the head. Below the arrow the neck and torso require 5 cm (2 in), and the legs a further 7.5 cm (3 in). The width of the outstretched arms is 15 cm (6 in) and is demarcated by arrows along the second horizontal line, parallel to the baseline.

5 With an old kitchen knife slice off thin slabs of wax from your block. Rub some barrier cream onto your hands, then start to knead the slabs in your hand.

6 You will quickly find that the heat from your hand makes the wax very malleable, soft and easy to manipulate.

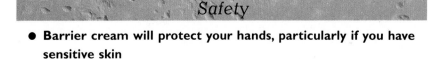

Safety

● **Barrier cream will protect your hands, particularly if you have sensitive skin**

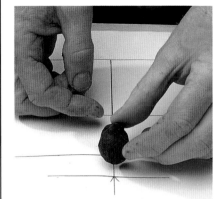

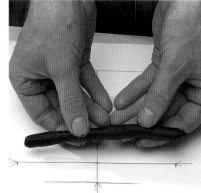

9 The torso, which uses the most wax, is measured and modelled in a similar fashion to the head. You now have six pieces of wax – a head, a torso, two arms and two legs. These need to be joined together to form a basic figure. ▼

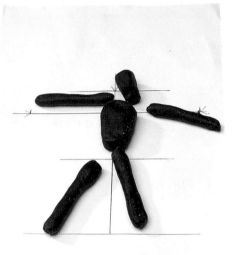

7 Begin by modelling the head, using your plan to determine the amount of wax needed for achieving its proper size. Then model the wax into a basic head shape.

8 Roll out a thin sausage of wax between your hands. Place this against the plan to determine the lengths of the arms. Once decided, split the sausage in two. Use the same technique to make two legs.

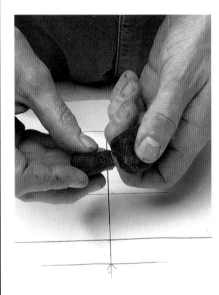

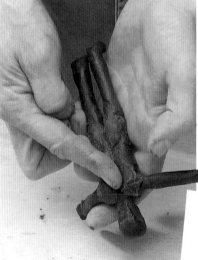

12 Lay your figure against the plan. As you can see, the priority has been to retain the measurements and thereby the proportions of the figure.

10 You will find that the wax has cooled, so gently knead the areas of wax to be joined on the head and torso until it again becomes soft. Push together and blend the wax until the two pieces join together.

11 Join the arms and legs to the torso using the same technique.

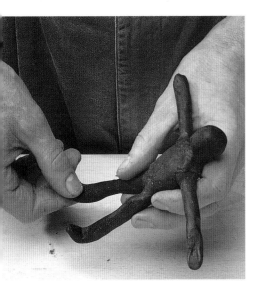

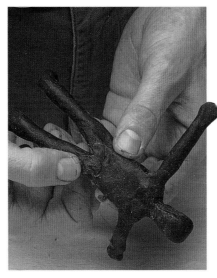

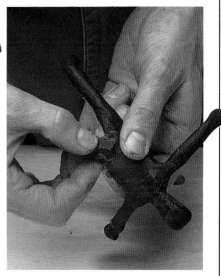

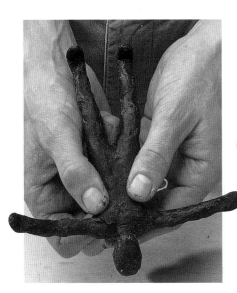

13 Pinch the end of each leg, let the wax soften and bend it at right angles to the leg to create feet.

14 Add small pieces of wax to the buttocks of the figure to give it more of an identity, without becoming involved in creating specific features.

15 Run your finger along the centre of the back, pushing down firmly to create shoulder blades. Add more pieces of wax until this area is fully modelled.

16 Turn the figure over and model the chest, arm and leg muscles. You will find that as you are turning the figure around in your hands the wax is really responsive to your touch, and can be further shaped and manipulated.

17 Here is a figure that is able to stand up on its own. Although no specific features have been modelled one is in no doubt at all that it is figurative. This is due to an adherence to the guideline proportions. Note how the hands have been squashed between thumb and forefinger.

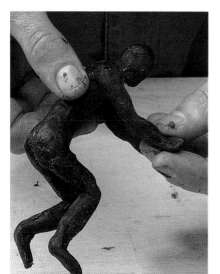

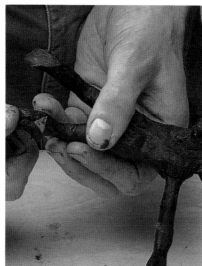

19 Any excess wax can be ◄ trimmed off with a modelling knife. This can also be used to give the legs and arms more shape.

20 Once the wax has cooled, this kneeling figure is hard and structurally sound. Together with the other kneeling figure it will become an integral part of the final sculptural configuration. ▼

18 Make five figures; bend two of them into a kneeling position. Just gently knead the part to be bent with your fingers, then bend it into place. Leave it to cool before you move on to the next bend.

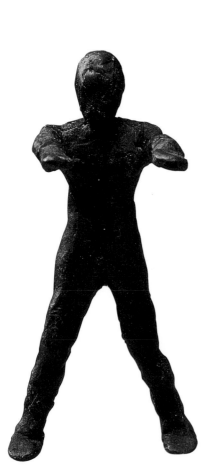

21 Make three standing figures, two with arms stretched forward and one with arms outstretched, following the method used for the kneeling figures.

22 Cover your modelling board with clingfilm and knead the wax until it is very soft. Start to create a wax base.

23 Continue building up the wax base, until it is 13 mm (½ in) thick. Make sure that you join soft wax to soft wax and push it together well to ensure a good join.

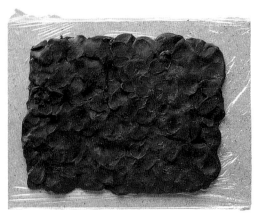

24 The wax base becomes an important structural component of the final sculpture, enabling it to stand upright.

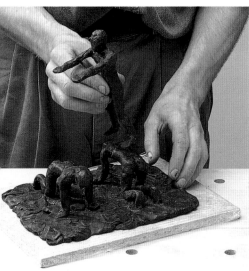

25 Join the two kneeling figures to the base using the same method as in step 10. Finally, join a standing figure onto the back of each kneeling one.

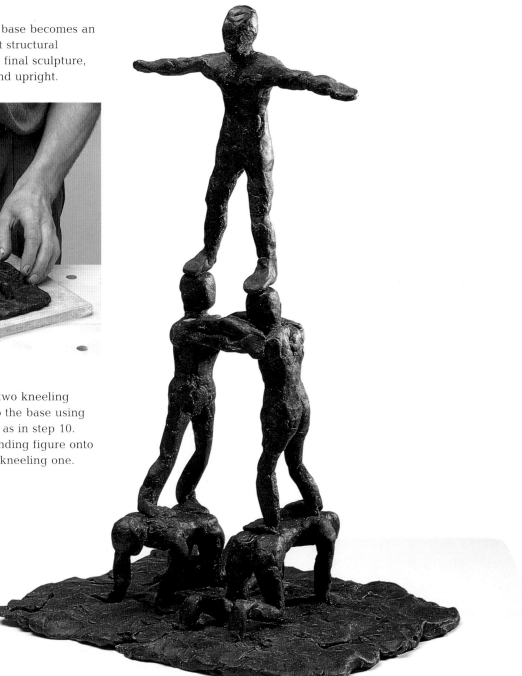

SEATED FIGURE

THE HUMAN FIGURE has always been one of sculpture's main subjects, from ancient times to the present day. However, it is very difficult to produce a visually acceptable figure at first try. So, at the outset, concentrate on modelling the forms of the figure in the correct proportions. Only then can you move on to model the specific parts of the figure in more detail, finally developing the skill to produce specific facial and bodily characteristics. Remember that the human figure is eminently recognizable – there will hardly be any doubt among viewers *what* your sculpture is. Too many specific details invariably lessen the impact of the sculpture; instead the eye focuses critically on those details which let the sculpture down.

In this project you will be modelling in clay, a traditional medium for figurative sculpture. The clay used is a self-hardening variety (available from any art/craft stockist) that dries very hard when exposed to air. Once dry, the clay can be coloured to produce an effect like that of a bronze sculpture.

The aim is to work within the confines and limitations of the material, choosing a pose that is easy to model and is self-supportive.

▲ Look at pictures of seated people and
◀ change the pose to suit your needs.
Hands and facial detail are often difficult for beginners, so this sculpture avoids them.

Materials

self-hardening clay
gold paint
white spirit
black acrylic paint

Equipment

sketch pad
pen
tape measure
lay figure
masking tape
**wood 5 × 5 × 8 cm (2 × 2
×3 in)**
card
clingfilm
rolling pin
modelling tool
water spray
sandpaper
modelling knife
paintbrush

Health/Safety

barrier cream
rubber gloves

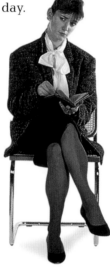

A wooden lay model will act as your guide to the pose and to the way various body parts relate to one another. ▶

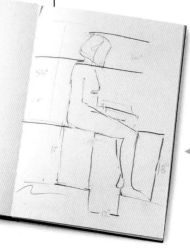

◀ Measurements, taken from a life model set up in the pose, are also extremely helpful. Sketches will help you to understand the pose and the various body parts.

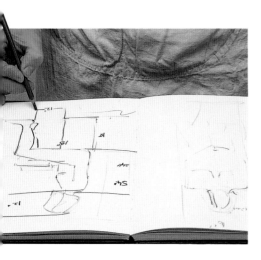

1 Place your model in the desired pose. Take measurements from the model and mark them on the drawings as you make them. The corresponding parts of the clay sculpture will be one-sixth of these measurements.

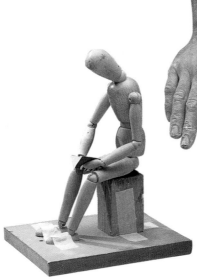

2 Set up your lay figure in the same pose as the life model and the proposed sculpture. Use masking tape to hold it in position, and a 5 × 5 × 7.5 cm (2 × 2 × 3 in) wood block as a seat. Fold a piece of card as a book.

3 Cover your modelling board with clingfilm. Roll out a slab of clay 1 cm (½ in) thick to cover the board.

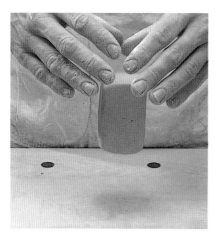

4 Roughly pummel a lump of clay into a cube 5 × 5 × 7.5 cm (2 × 2 × 3 in). Consolidate the shape into a cube by dropping each side alternately onto the work surface.

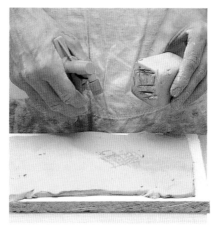

5 Score the underside of the cube with your modelling tool, as well as an area of the clay base. Moisten both areas with water.

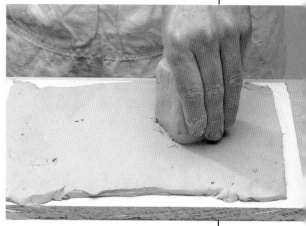

6 Push the cube down onto the base and twist it round so that the water is pushed out. The sides of the cube should be parallel with the sides of the modelling board.

Safety

- **Barrier cream will protect your hands, particularly if you have sensitive skin**
- **Use rubber gloves when painting**

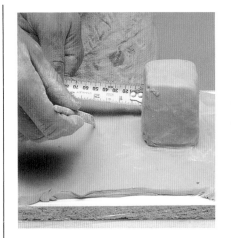

7 Run your modelling tool around the junction of the cube and base to blend the edges together. Measure and mark a line on the base 5 cm (2 in) in from the front of the cube.

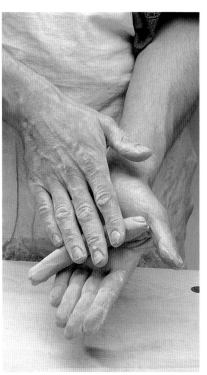

8 In the palms of your hands roll two sausages of clay until they are 18 cm (7 in) long. These are the legs of the sculpture. Bend the sausages at right angles in the middle, and bend a 2.5 cm (1 in) long segment at right angles on both for the feet.

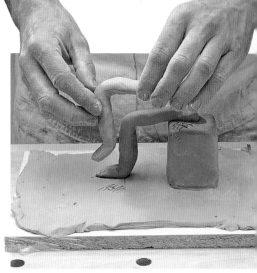

9 Join the feet to the base, making sure that the heel rests on the line already drawn. Join the other ends of the sausages onto the plinth. When joining clay to clay in this manner score, wet and push well home, as in step 6.

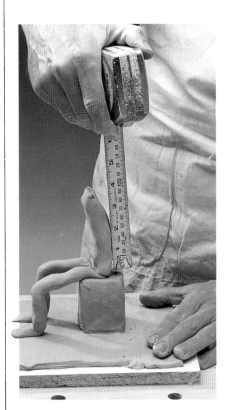

10 Join a cylinder of clay, 10 cm (4 in) high, to the top of the legs and the seat forming the torso. Bend it slightly forward.

11 Trim the excess clay on the base to create an area approximately 19 × 10 cm (7½ × 4 in).

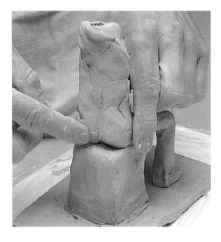

12 Begin modelling the buttocks, always adding one small piece of clay at a time.

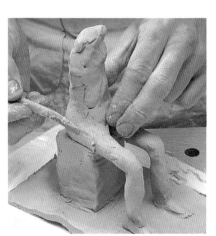

13 The modelling tool is especially useful when shaping the rounded forms of the legs.

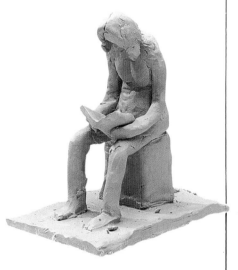

14 The back and the top half of the figure now have a recognizable shape and the sculpture is starting to look human. Continue to shape the front of the torso.

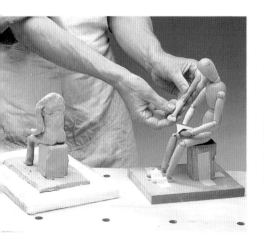

15 Roll out a thin sausage of clay. Place it against the arm of the lay figure to check the configuration of the clay, then join the clay arm onto the torso of the sculpture.

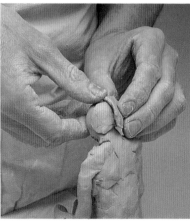

16 Take up a ball of clay for the head. Mould it into a basic oval shape and add it to the torso. Cover with a thin slab of clay for the hair.

17 The constituent parts of the sculpture are now in place. The front of the torso has been modelled into shape, a book has been added, and the hair has been shaped to fall over the face.

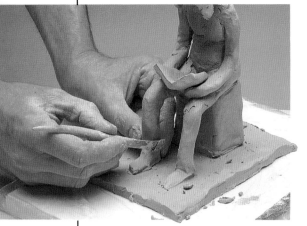

18 Use your modelling tool to finalize the shape of the sculpture. Reduce the clay around the legs by slicing it away and model a simple foot shape.

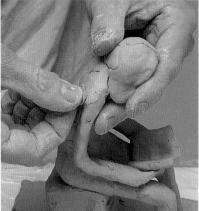

19 Blend in the clay on the hair by smoothing over with your modelling tool. Add small pieces of clay to give more shape to the shoulders and arms.

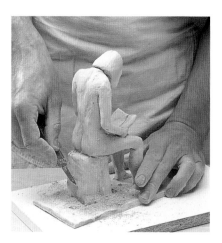

20 Leave the sculpture uncovered for 48 hours to dry out. Remove the clingfilm from the board. Using a modelling knife, smooth away some of the inconsistencies on the clay surface of the seat.

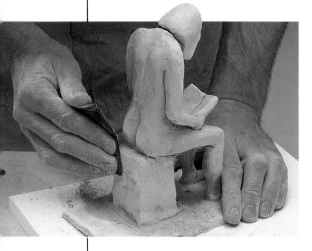

21 Sandpaper smooth the surface of the base and seat.

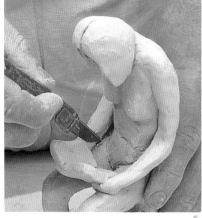

22 Use the knife on other parts of the figure to cut away small lumps of clay or inconsistencies in the surface. Finish off with sandpaper.

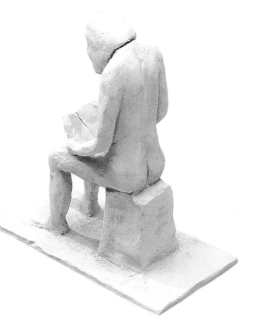

23 The sculpture is now in its finished dried clay state. Even without an understanding of anatomy, it has been possible to create a recognizable figurative sculpture.

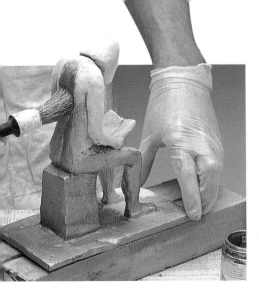

24 Paint a coat of gold enamel over the whole sculpture and leave to dry. Wash the brush out with white spirit.

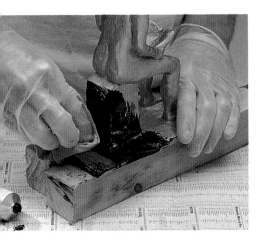

25 Brush black acrylic paint over the gold and leave to dry for a few minutes. Then wipe away with a cloth, leaving the black paint trapped in the crevices of the sculpture. Wash the brush out with water.

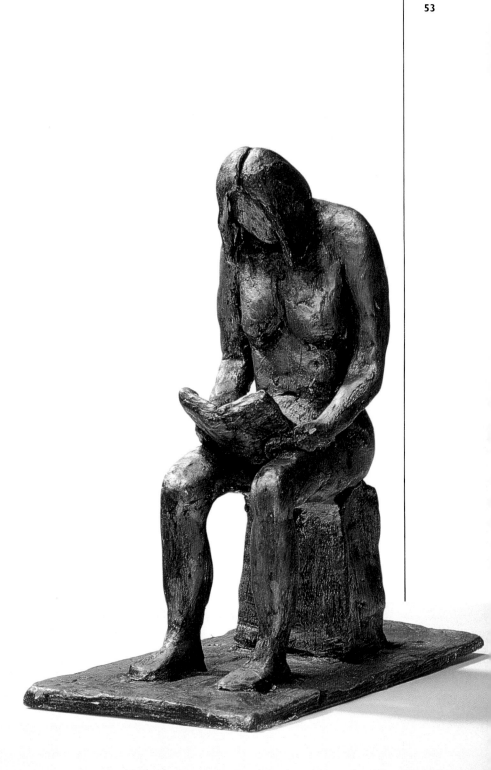

MUD AND STRAW DOG

T HE CRUDE COMBINATION of mud and straw is one of the most effective building materials known. Extremely hard-wearing, it has provided shelter through the ages to the present day in a variety of cultures. This marriage of materials, once dry, is extremely strong and, of course, very cheap.

In this project you will be making a permanent sculptural form, which can be placed outside in a rural or garden setting. When envisioning such a sculpture, the location, choice of material and the form the sculpture will take are of paramount importance. You need to achieve a harmonious relationship among all three.

Even though you are using an unorthodox material, you still have to address the important sculptural issue of the armature. You will need to design and make an armature that will provide an adequate support for the material and whose form closely resembles the form of the proposed sculpture. First, make a "dummy" armature. This will alert you to any changes that may be necessary. In this case, it was necessary to add a small length of wood at the top of each of the front legs, so that they could be joined to the shoulder piece.

The armature is made from lengths of wood to produce a basic skeletal structure. Chicken wire is then stretched over the top of this, and pushed and squeezed into the required form. The interior is filled with straw to help support the weight of the modelling medium.

▲ If you can't make drawings from life, photographs are more than adequate – and at least they won't move or walk away!

Materials

strips of MDF board
300 × 2.5 × 2.5 cm
(120 × 1 × 1 in) piece of
wood
4 cm (1½ in) oval nails
chicken wire
mud
straw

Equipment

sketchbook
paper
pencil
glue gun
all-purpose glue sticks
saw
hammer
wire cutters
pliers

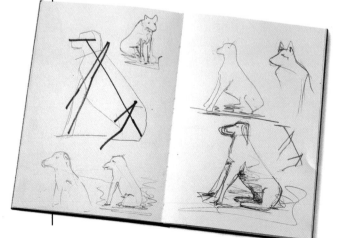

◀ Initial drawings will help you to understand the pose. This, in turn, will help you to plan a suitable armature.

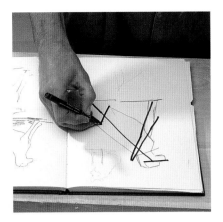

1 Draw the dog in an upright sitting position; over this draw the proposed shape of the armature.

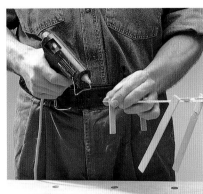

2 With the glue gun join together strips of MDF wood to produce a small version of the armature.

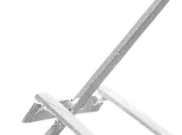

3 Although clumsy looking, this model of the armature can give you an idea as to whether it will work out if made larger. ▼

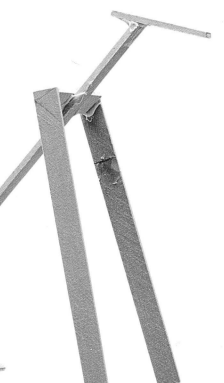

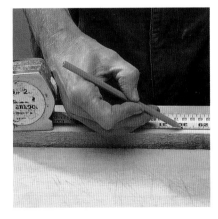

4 Take measurements from this model. Multiply them by three to calculate the dimensions of an armature three times the size of the model.

5 Transfer these scaled-up measurements to the 2.5 × 2.5 cm (1 × 1 in) wood and saw to length the required number of pieces: one at 75 cm (30 in), two at 20 cm (8 in), one at 30 cm (12 in), one at 45 cm (18 in), two at 23 cm (9 in), and two at 7.5 cm (3 in).

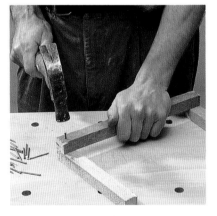

6 Nail the 30 cm (12 in) length onto the two 20 cm (8 in) lengths to produce the hind-quarters.

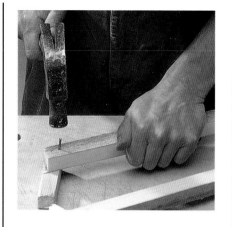

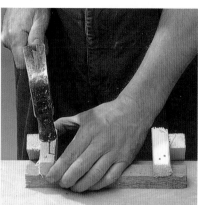

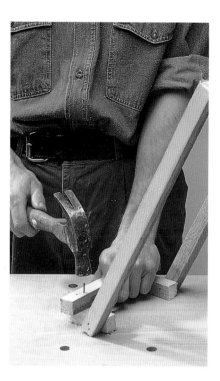

7 Nail the two 7.5 cm (3 in) lengths onto the end of each of the 45 cm (18 in) lengths at an angle of approximately 45°.

8 Nail the other end of these two short pieces to the 23 cm (9 in) length. This will support the front legs and shoulders. Note how it is necessary to let the legs hang down over the front of the work surface.

9 In all cases in which you nail two pieces of wood together, turn the joined wood over and nail again from the other side to ensure a strong fixing.

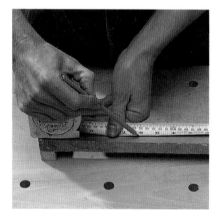

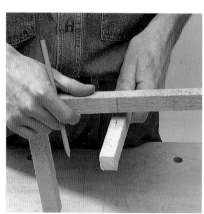

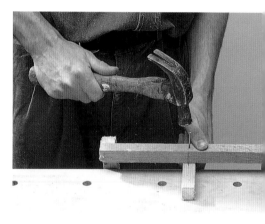

10 Mark the centre point on the hindquarters and then mark the point on the spine 7.5 cm (3 in) up from the bottom.

11 Match these two marks up and hold the two sticks in place. Position the end of the spine on the work surface with the hindquarters right up against the front of the work surface.

12 Nail the hindquarters to the spine, making sure that the two centre lines are matched up.

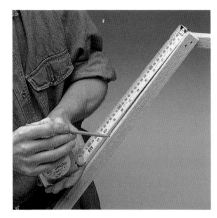

13 Nail the remaining 23 cm (9 in) length onto the other end of the spine. Measure down from the top of the spine 25 cm (10 in) and mark the centre point. Mark the centre point on the shoulders and nail onto the spine, making sure that the centre marks are lined up.

14 The finished wooden armature with the third size model. Notice how it was necessary to add a piece of wood at the top of the front legs to enable them to be joined to the shoulders.

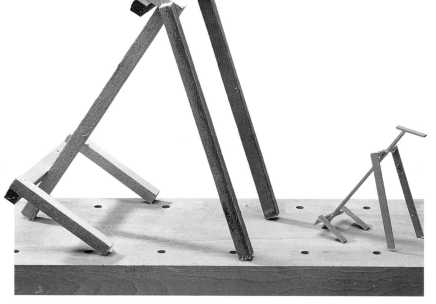

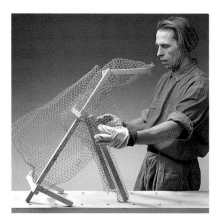

15 Wrap chicken wire around the head of the armature, pushing it tightly together to hold it in place. Continue to wrap the wire around the main body of the sculpture.

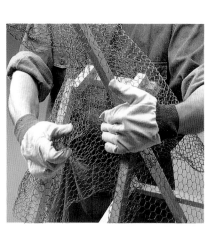

16 Push and manipulate the chicken wire all the way around so that it imitates the form of a dog as nearly as possible.

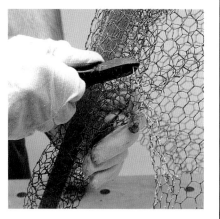

17 Cut the chicken wire with wire cutters, leaving enough to wrap around the front legs.

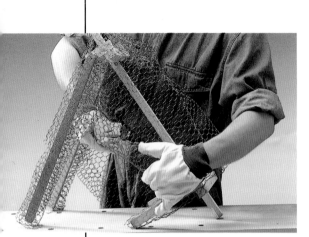

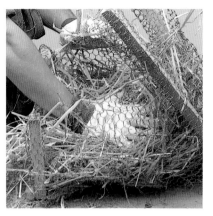

18 With the front legs covered, push the wire into and around the hindquarters.

19 Before finally joining the chicken wire up underneath the dog, stuff the interior with straw, packing it in as tightly as possible.

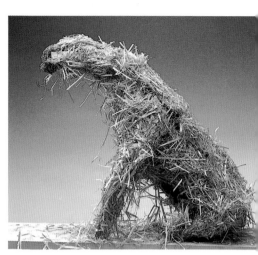

20 The armature is now ready. Even in this state it has quite a discernible dog form. You have achieved one of the objectives.

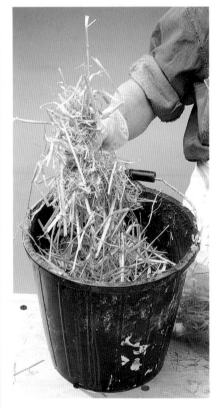

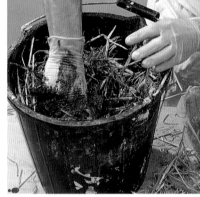

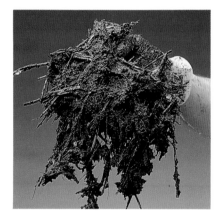

22 Mix the straw well into the mud so that it is evenly distributed throughout the mud.

23 This is the consistency of mix that you are aiming for. It should not be wet and runny, though it also should not be too dry.

21 To a half full bucket of mud, add a few handfuls of straw.

24 Taking a handful at a time, start packing the mix tightly over the surface of the armature. At the same time keep to the "doggy" form of the sculpture.

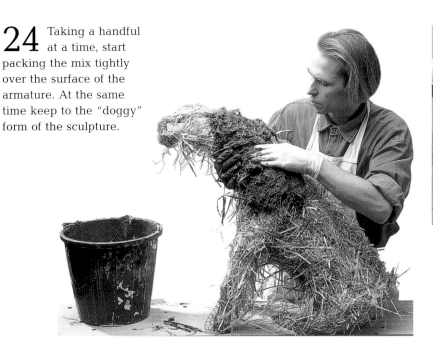

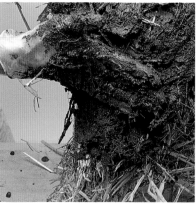

25 When applying the mix it is essential that you pack it tightly so that it integrates fully with the chicken wire and straw. This is especially true on vertical areas.

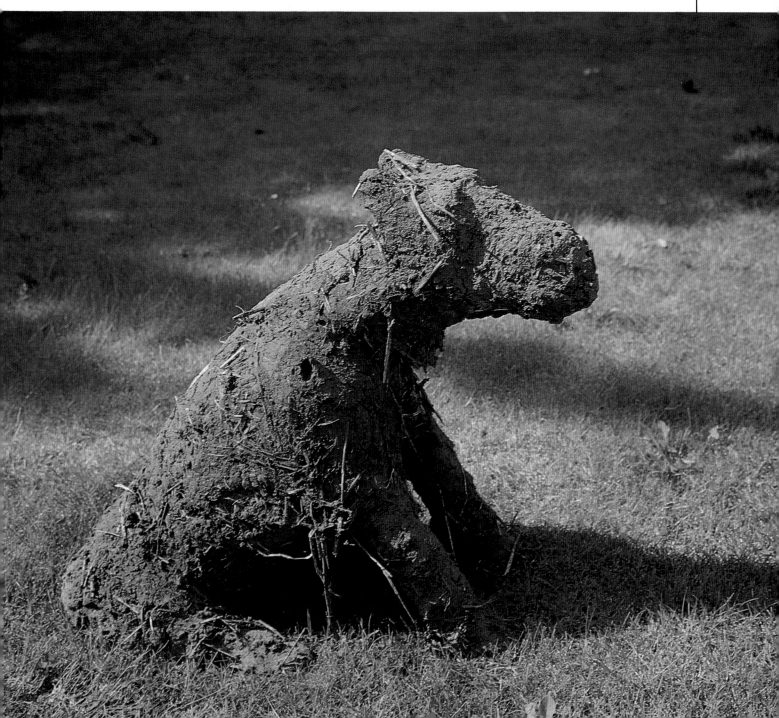

GRAVITY

THE FORCE OF GRAVITY cannot be ignored and a sculpture that seemingly defies gravity is a very powerful sculptural statement. Getting a sculpture to stay in its intended position is a common problem faced by sculptors and there are a variety of ways to deal with the effect of gravity. The sculptures in this section are examples of how this problem has been resolved in an efficient and unobtrusive way.

An armature provides a foundation to which material can be applied to develop the form of the sculpture. If the armature is carefully planned parts of, or the whole of, the sculpture can give the impression of defying gravity and sometimes the use of a base is crucial. A base could also simply hold a sculpture or its component forms in a gravity-defying position. Of course the base also serves the more utilitarian function of displaying a sculpture to its best effect.

The format of a carved sculpture can be determined by the way a block of material sits comfortably. Similarly, a constructed sculpture uses the structural qualities of its various parts to support each other and the sculpture as a whole.

▲ **Amanda Lorens**
BATEAU DE FRUITS

This sculpture was inspired by a ferry journey from England to France. It uses a steel armature, some of which is left exposed, to which plaster and straw have been added to create the boat and fruit forms. Thus a sculpture has been created which is firmly rooted to gravity but contained within it are parts which defy gravity.
91.5 cm (36 in) high

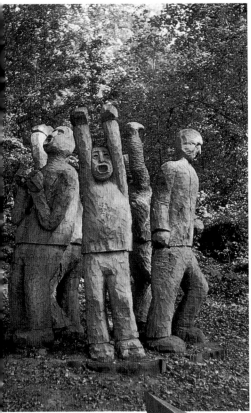

Robert Koenig
RUSTIC DANCE

Each of the five figures in this dynamic carved wood sculpture have a base that is integral to the tree trunk from which they were carved. A combination of the base and their vertical configuration enable them to stand up.
Over life size

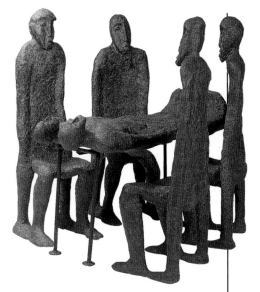

Mark D Chatterley
THE SIN EATERS

This grouping of fired clay figures invokes a real sense of drama. Notice how the chair on each of the seated figures becomes both a structural and a compositional device which allows each of the figures to exist within the sculpture. This is also a good example of how a figure can be modelled without getting bogged down in detail.
1.4 × 1.8 × 1.8 m
(4½ × 6 × 6 ft)

Sophie Ryder
DANCING HARES

In this sculpture the artist exploits the structural qualities of wire, together with the naturalistic dancing configurations of hares to enable the sculpture to support itself.
1.7 × 1.7 m (5½ × 5½ ft)

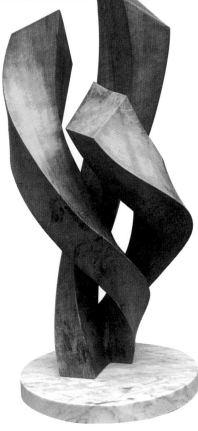

Dick Onians
THREE ASPIRING

The carved holly forms defy gravity as they soar upwards and around each other, giving a real sense of movement. This is made possible by the marble base.
61 × 26.5 cm (24 × 10½ in)

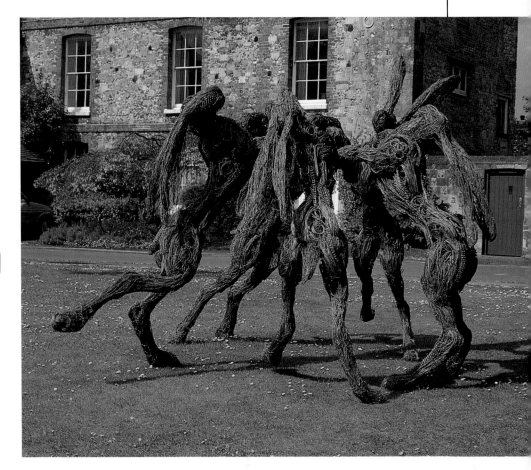

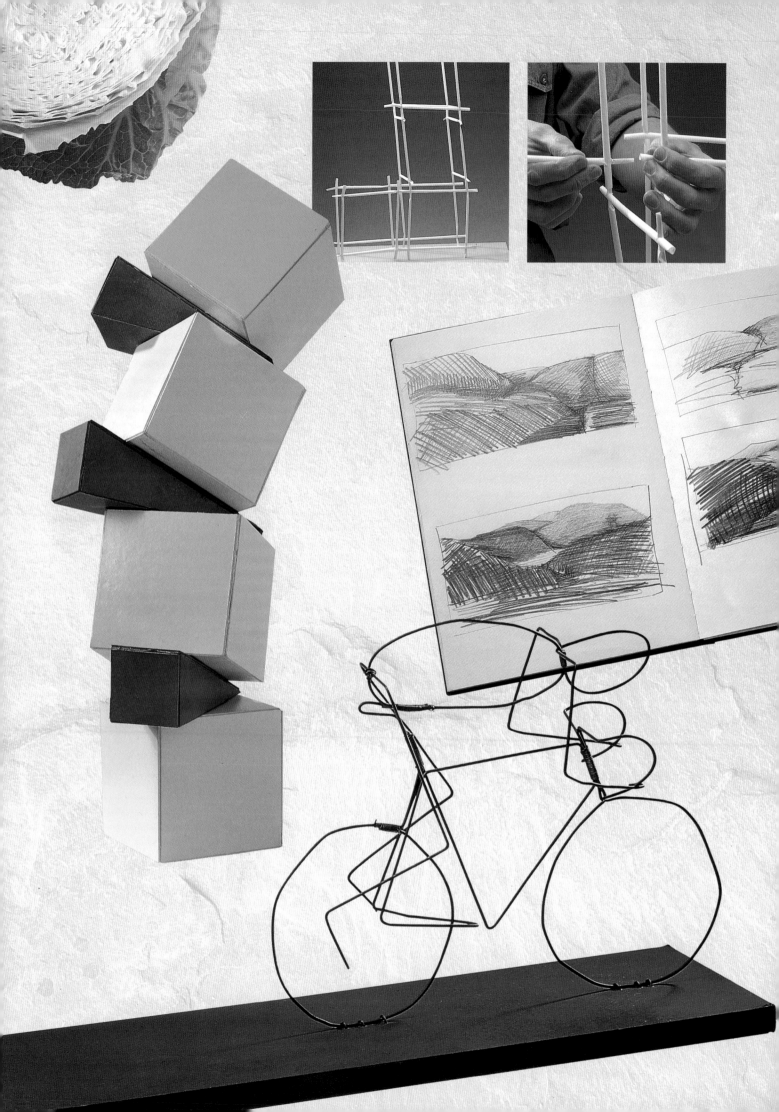

3

CONSTRUCTION

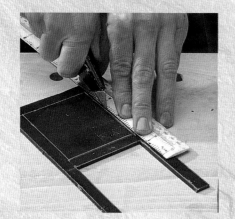

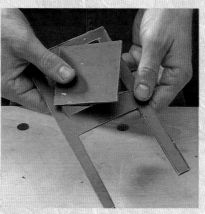

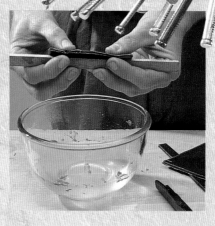

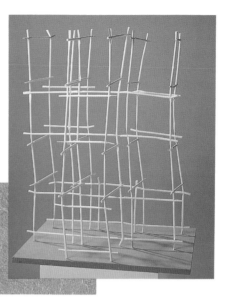

ARCHITECTURAL TOWER

Unlike the other projects, this sculpture is not meant to last. But this in no way devalues its importance. The project should enable you to understand how to build a stable structure. Issues of strength and stability are fundamental to the nature of sculpture and are relevant to all types of sculpture, be it carving, modelling or construction. Before embarking on making a sculpture, especially one needing an armature, strength and stability is something you should always consider. Search out open structures built using a basic geometric unit, such as a square or triangle, which is repeated over and over again in the structure, providing the necessary support.

Since this is a learning project, do not expect success at first go or at every stage. In fact the more failures you have the more you learn – you could even say the project becomes more successful. Your aim is to find a way to join paper straws together to produce geometric units. These units will be used to build a stable structure. This is not an easy task, but because the straws are relatively inexpensive, it means that you do not have to be sparing about using them. You can be adventurous, exploring all the possibilities inherent in creating vertical structures. Once you have found a combination of straws which can be interlocked and repeated to make a structure, see how high you are able to go before it begins to collapse. The particular unit shown here is one of many options – try to find your own. Remember that no extra aid can be used to join or fix the straws together.

▼ Before starting, spend some time looking at steel constructions such as the Eiffel Tower, bridges and even scaffolding around buildings undergoing renovation.

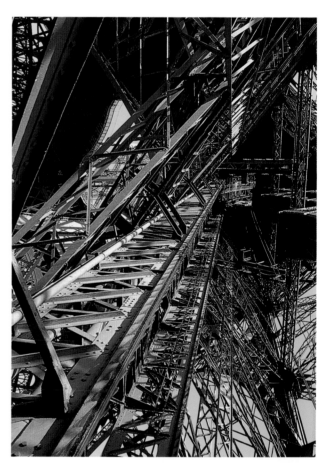

Materials

art straws

Equipment

ruler
scissors

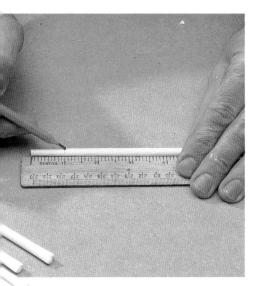

1 Make a mark 2.5 cm (1 in) in at each end of the straw.

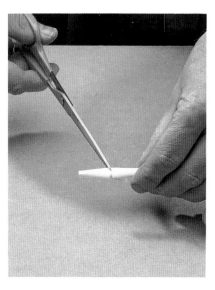

2 Along this mark cut out two small wedge-shaped openings opposite one another.

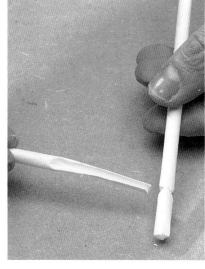

3 For each unit you need two ordinary straws and two with openings cut into each end.

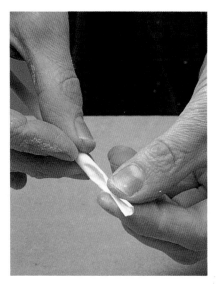

4 Take the two ordinary straws and pinch each of the four ends.

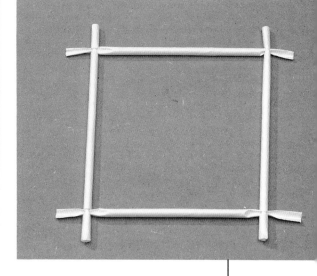

5 Push a pinched end into the opening of one of the cut straws. Repeat at the other end. Push the other two pinched ends into the cuts in the other straw.

6 Notice how the pinched straw has been pushed in approximately 2.5 cm (1 in), and the end splayed out a bit. You should make a number of these units before going on to the next step.

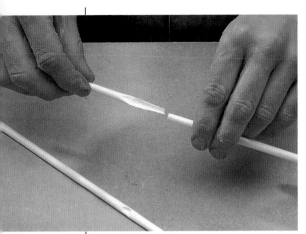

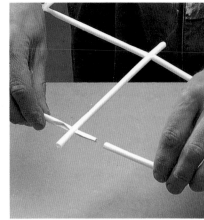

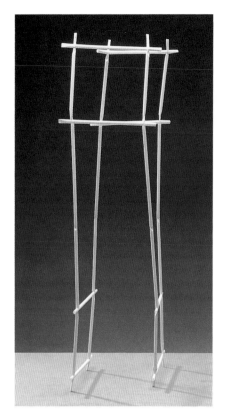

7 To make a longer straw, pinch together one end of a straw and place in the end of another ordinary straw. Make two of these longer straws.

8 Fix the two elongated straws onto the ends of one of the square units. Fix another unit onto the other ends of the elongated straws, at right angles to the unit at the other end.

9 So far the partial structure can stand vertically, though rather unsurely.

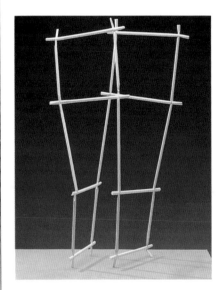

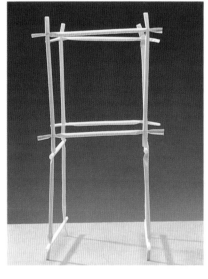

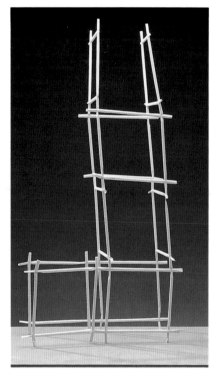

10 Reducing the elongated straws by one does not improve the stability of the structure.

11 By turning the second two units at right angles to the first, the structure is on a much more sound footing.

12 By continuing to alternate the units at right angles to each other you can begin building a tall structure. Extending the structure horizontally along the base also gives more stability.

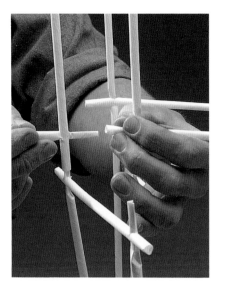

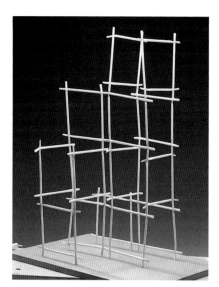

13 Continue to build vertically, while at the same time continuing to join units together horizontally. ◀

14 By increasing the base area you can continue to build more storeys onto your structure. ▶

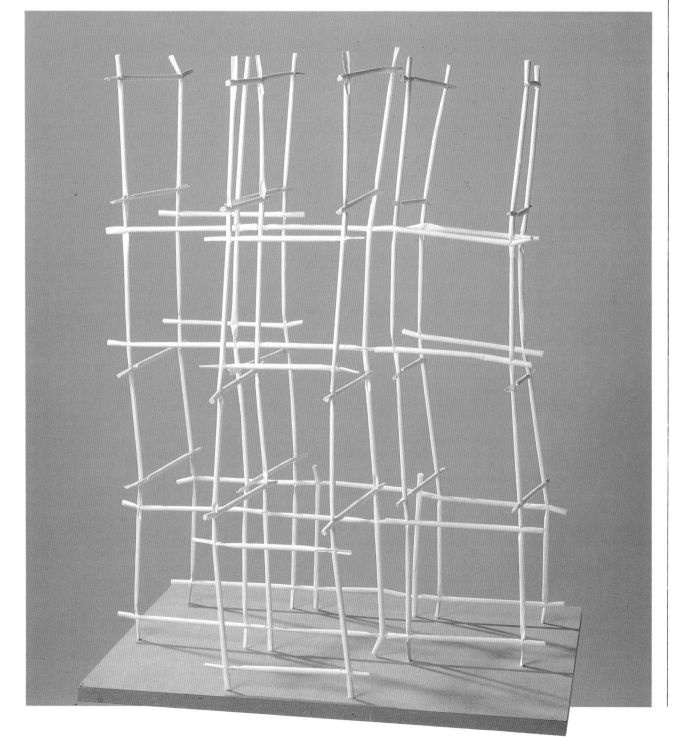

GEOMETRIC FORMS

T HE WORD "GEOMETRY" invariably conjures up the specialized worlds of mathematics and science. But you have only to look around to see what an important part it plays in the natural world. For instance, look closely at the way leaves are distributed around a branch on a tree. You will be able to identify a definite system of order. Look, too, at the human figure; its constituent forms can be reduced to geometric shapes. It is also useful to appreciate how geometry is used in our built environment. Look at architecture, shelving units, furniture, and the rest of our constructed surroundings.

This project investigates the role that geometry can play in deciding the form and composition of a sculpture. It also introduces you to the construction technique of sculpture-making. The basic raw material needed is a sheet of card or something flat (two-dimensional), from which you can construct something in the round (three-dimensional). You must make a paper template first to ensure that the shapes fold together properly before you draw them onto card.

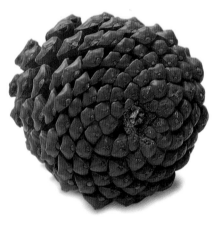

▲ Explore the geometry in natural forms. Note the spiral arrangement of a cabbage or a pine cone, for example.

A wedge and a cube have been chosen quite specifically for this project. The cube is a stable object, able to sit on any of its faces and not move. The wedge, on the other hand, although capable of standing on its own, can also be seen as a disruptive element. These two forms are alternatively stacked until no more can be added without causing a collapse. Blue gives weight to the wedge while the yellow makes the cube seem lighter and so more likely to be unbalanced.

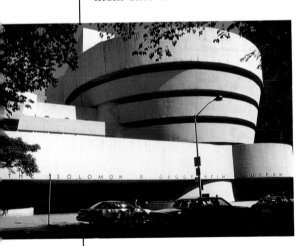

▲ The Guggenheim Museum in New York is an excellent example of a building that is based on geometric forms. In this case, the inspiration was the spiral of a shell.

Materials

card
yellow spray paint
blue spray paint

Equipment

paper
drawing board
set square
craft knife
metal ruler
masking tape
glue gun
all-purpose glue sticks
newspaper

Health/Safety

rubber gloves
respirator mask

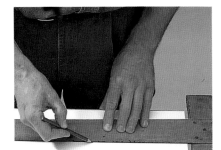

1 Place the card on your drawing board and draw a horizontal line close to the bottom edge of your card. Place your square along the top end of the card and draw a vertical line that terminates at the beginning of and at right angles to the horizontal line.

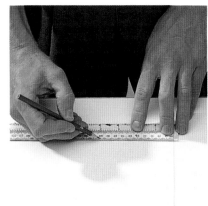

2 From this vertical line measure into the card and mark the 10cm (4in) point. Still with your square at the top edge of the card, line up the straight edge with this 10cm (4in) mark and draw another vertical line.

3 Along one of the vertical lines mark four points, leaving 10cm (4in) between each, starting from your horizontal base line. With your square along the left hand edge of the card draw horizontal lines at these marks, joining the two vertical lines, and at the second and third marks extend the horizontal line further across the card.

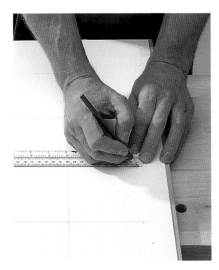

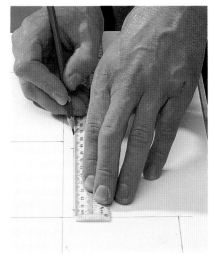

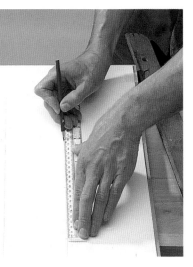

4 You now have a configuration not unlike a cross. Mark a point on one of the horizontal lines 10cm (4in) either side of each vertical line. Place your square at the top of the card, line it up with the marks, and draw a vertical line to join the two horizontal lines.

5 Draw a border, measured 1cm (½in) outside, around the outer perimeter of the two bottom squares. Draw another 1cm (½in) border along the two top edges of the side squares. Finally measure, mark and draw a diagonal line at each corner of this border, 1cm (½in) in from each end.

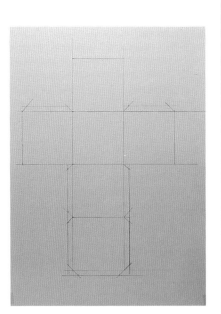

6 The plan of the cube is now drawn out. The six sides of the cube are apparent, each measuring 10 × 10cm (4 × 4in), with flanges attached to some sides to facilitate easy fixing.

Safety

- **Use spray paint outdoors or in a well ventilated area**
- **Make sure that all surrounding areas are covered with newspaper**
- **Wear rubber gloves and a respirator mask**

7 Place a metal ruler along the exterior lines drawn on the card and cut the plan of the box out from the sheet. Remember to hold the ruler and your knife firm to ensure that you get a nice clean cut.

8 When the plan of the box has been cut from the card, note the diagonals at the end of each flange have also been cut away. The inner pencil lines delineate the six faces of the cube.

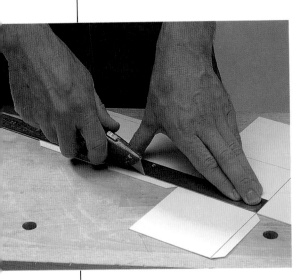

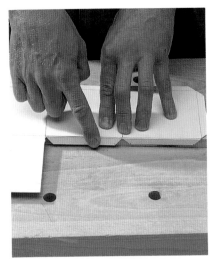

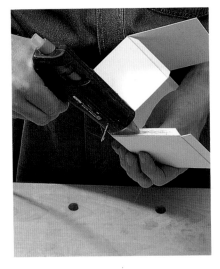

9 The next job is to bend the flanges at right angles to each of the faces. The faces, in turn, should be bent at right angles to each other. This is done by scoring the card with the craft knife. Place the metal ruler along an inner pencil line. Run the knife along the straight edge, applying just enough pressure to cut halfway through the card. Be careful *not* to cut all the way through. Score all drawn lines this way.

10 Now bend the flanges. First place the card on a length of timber, lining up the scored line with the top edge of the wood. Push the flanges down – you will find they take the new position very easily. Do the same with the faces of the cube.

11 With all the faces and flanges bent at right angles, apply glue to one of the flanges on the face that has three flanges.

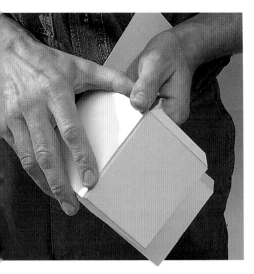

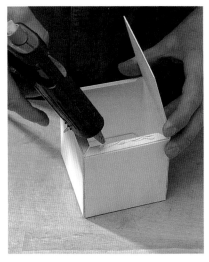

12 Quickly position this flange behind its adjacent face, making sure that you line it up properly. Hold it in place until the glue has set. Apply glue to the opposite flange and stick this to the opposite face of the cube.

13 There are now three flanges left. Apply glue to all three. Push down the top face, lining it up with the other three faces of the cube, and hold it in place until the glue has set.

14 Construct the wedge ▷ shape in the same way as the cube. Here is the plan drawn on the card, in which five faces are marked out. The central column is 5cm (2in) wide, divided into three sections, 5cm (2in), 15cm (6in) and 16cm (6¼in) in length, the longest at the top. Extend the baseline of the middle section 5cm (2in) either side of the column. Draw a diagonal from each end of this line to the top of the middle section. Add flanges 1cm (½in) wide along these diagonal faces and at the top.

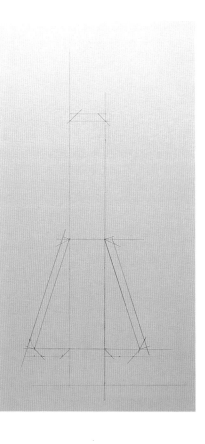

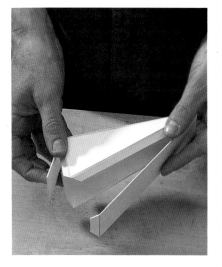

16 Score the lines along the edge of the faces, as with the cube. Bend the flanges round at right angles. Apply glue along one of the diagonal flanges, position it and glue the top wedge-shaped flap in place.

15 Here is the plan of the wedge cut from the card. Pay attention to the drawn lines that need to be scored with the metal ruler and the craft knife.

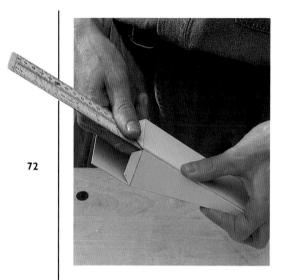

17 Apply glue to the diagonal flange. Position it underneath the top flap, with a ruler placed inside and pressing up against the flange to hold it in place until the glue sets. Apply glue to the three flanges at the end of the wedge, fold the end over and hold in place until the glue sets.

18 The finished wedge and cube shapes. For this project you need to make three wedge shapes and four cube shapes. ▼

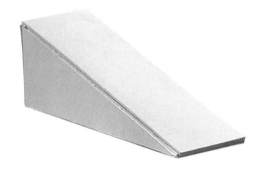

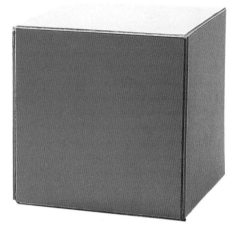

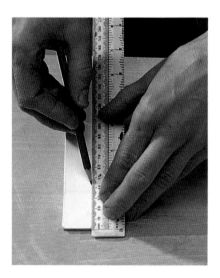

19 On each of the wedges measure and then draw a line down the centre of the sloping face.

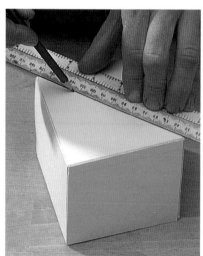

20 Draw a diagonal across the top of each cube.

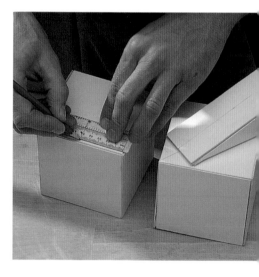

21 Place a wedge on the top of the cube. Line up the end of the centre line on the wedge with the diagonal line on top of the cube.

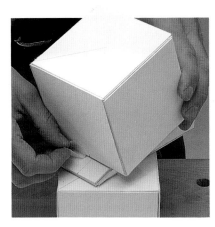

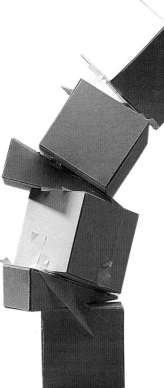

22 On the front face of each subsequent cube, mark the centre point along the bottom edge. Place another cube on top of the wedge, lining up this mark with the centre line on the wedge. You will need to use masking tap to hold these temporarily in place.

23 Here is the final ▶ sculpture, with each of the elements held temporarily in place with masking tape. You will notice how the sculpture has developed a spiral movement.

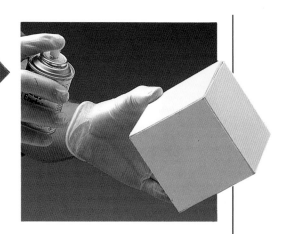

24 Before the final fixing, spray the cubes yellow and the wedges blue. Protect surrounding areas with newspaper.

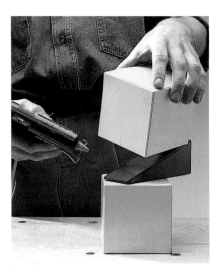

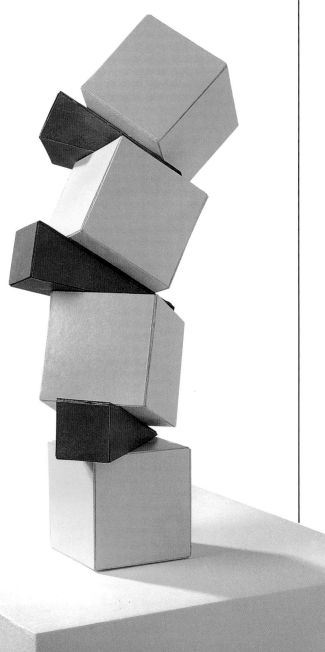

25 When the cubes and wedges are sprayed, fix them together with the glue gun in the same position as before. Use the same marks you made previously to glue and position the elements. Mask off adjacent areas with masking tape and newspaper and then spray paint to cover any pencil marks.

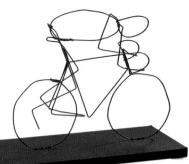

RACING CYCLIST

T HE MATERIAL YOU choose can have a strong determining effect on the type of form the final sculpture has. The base, too, can be used to elicit a particular response from the viewer. In this project you address both of these issues.

A base can be purely functional, holding a sculpture firmly in a particular position. It can display a sculpture to its best advantage or it may become an integral part of the sculptural composition. Its perimeters define the area within which the sculpture stands. The size and shape of the base and the positioning of the sculpture on it can radically alter the meaning of a sculpture. For instance, a large base supporting a small figure may transform a straightforward figurative sculpture into a statement about loneliness and alienation.

An appreciation of the qualities and potential of the material you are using is always an important aspect when beginning a sculpture. In this project you will be using coathanger wire. It has a certain amount of structural strength, but is easily bent and shaped, and can be joined using binding wire. When bending the wire, only use one hanger-length for each section of the sculpture as the less joining of parts, the stronger it will be. The cyclist invokes a sense of movement on its own, but placing it at the end of a long thin base really accentuates this feeling.

Painting the cyclist and base a uniform colour imposes a visual unity as well as covering the binding wire and staples.

▲ A subject like this requires a certain amount of preplanning. Start by making drawings from cycles and from photographs of racing cyclists.

▲ It is best to make simplified line drawings. You will find it interesting to note how the drawn line corresponds to the wire as it takes on its shape.

Materials

binding wire
masking tape
wire coathangers
clear adhesive tape
wooden base
netting staples
black spray paint

Equipment

pencil
sketchbook
wire cutters
pliers
hammer

Health/Safety

rubber gloves
respirator mask

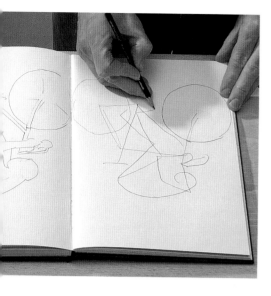

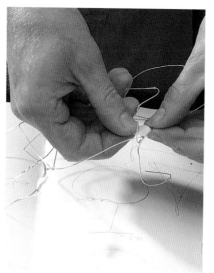

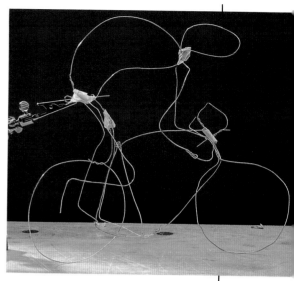

1 Choose the preliminary sketch of a cyclist which pleases you most and make a simplified line drawing from it, bearing in mind that the sculpture based on it will be made from wire.

2 Taking your drawing as a base, use binding wire to work out the most efficient way to create the shape of the cyclist and his cycle. When you have arrived at the best method of bending the wire, make a note of the configuration, section by section, in your sketchbook.

3 Bind the wire parts together with masking tape. This will give you an indication as to how the sculpture will look.

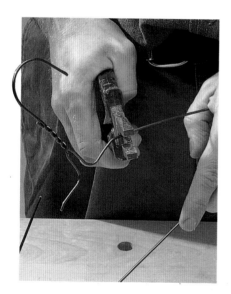

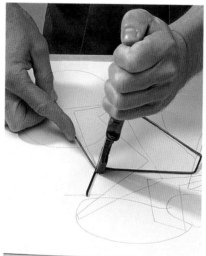

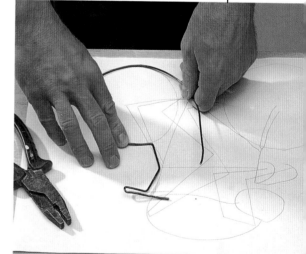

4 Prepare five coathangers by cutting off the hanging hook and bending each hanger straight with pliers.

Safety

- **Use spray paint outdoors or in a well ventilated area**
- **Make sure that all surrounding areas are covered with newspaper**
- **Wear rubber gloves and a respirator mask**

5 Using the simplified line drawing, begin bending the wire into the shape of the bicycle frame. Refer to the sketch made in step 2. Use pliers to hold the wire steady while you bend it into shape with your other hand.

6 The pliers are necessary to bend and shape the saddle, but the wheel can be bent into position with your hands.

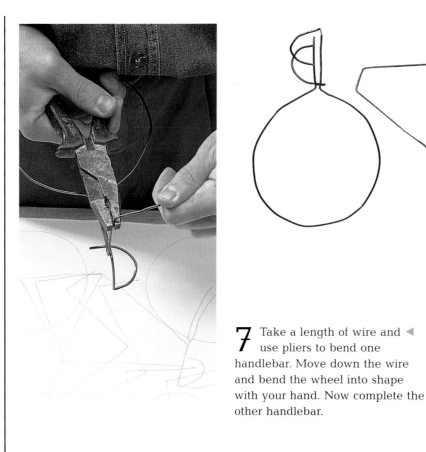

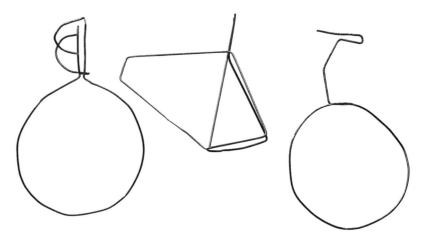

7 Take a length of wire and ◀ use pliers to bend one handlebar. Move down the wire and bend the wheel into shape with your hand. Now complete the other handlebar.

8 Now the three parts of the bicycle have been bent into position. Note how there is no overlapping of the wire along its length.

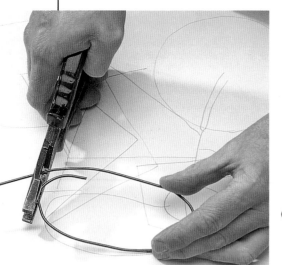

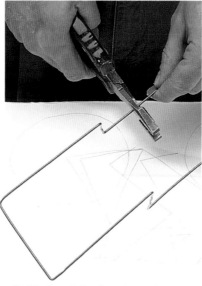

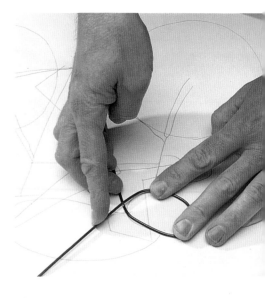

9 Using your drawing as a guide, bend the torso into shape with your hand. Cut off the excess wire with pliers.

10 Bend the legs into shape with pliers, starting in the middle of a length. Cut off the excess with pliers to form the feet.

11 Starting in the middle of a length of wire and using the drawing as a guide, bend the wire round to create the head.

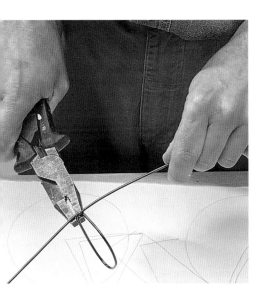

13 The three parts of the body, bent in position, are now ready to be joined together.

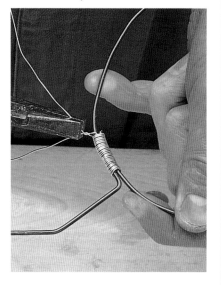

12 Using pliers, twist the head round at right angles to the shoulders. Use the pliers to bend the wire at right angles to form the shoulders and the elbows.

14 Use clear adhesive tape to hold the two parts together.

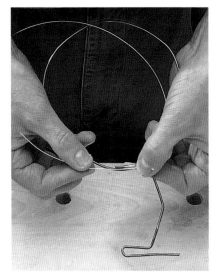

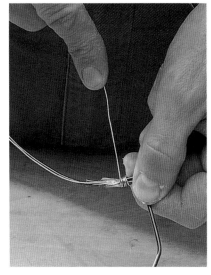

15 Lay a straight length of binding wire along the join of the thicker hanger wire, making sure that a short length, about 7.5cm (3in), goes beyond the area to be joined.

16 Wrap more wire tightly around the join of the two parts of the cycle. Continue to wrap the wire over the straight length of binding wire already there. Wrap the wire neatly, and avoid crossing over a piece of wire that has previously been wrapped around.

17 When you get to the end of the join there will be two ends of wire. Finish them off by twisting with the pliers. Cut off excess wire. Continue to assemble the bicycle by joining on the third section with bending wire.

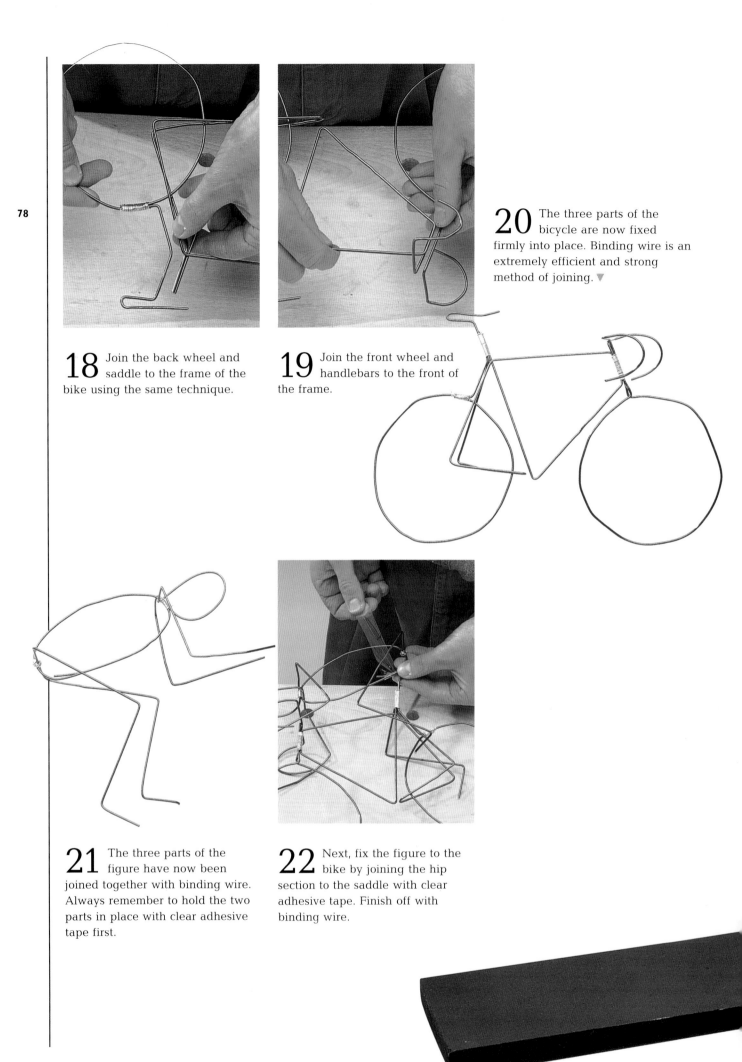

18 Join the back wheel and saddle to the frame of the bike using the same technique.

19 Join the front wheel and handlebars to the front of the frame.

20 The three parts of the bicycle are now fixed firmly into place. Binding wire is an extremely efficient and strong method of joining. ▼

21 The three parts of the figure have now been joined together with binding wire. Always remember to hold the two parts in place with clear adhesive tape first.

22 Next, fix the figure to the bike by joining the hip section to the saddle with clear adhesive tape. Finish off with binding wire.

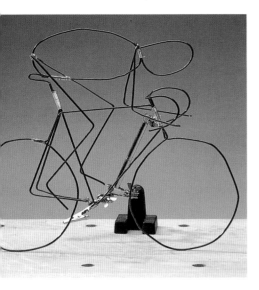 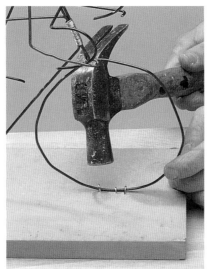 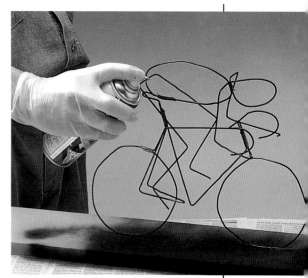

23 The figure is now solidly astride the bike. Note how the ends of each arm have been bent and then wrapped around the handlebars.

24 Mark the centre line of your base with a pencil. Position the cycle along this line so that the front wheel is placed as far as possible along the end of this line toward the front of the base. Use a hammer to bang in netting staples to traverse the wire of the wheels. This will hold the cyclist firmly in a vertical position.

25 Put on rubber gloves and a face mask for protection. Mask surrounding areas with newspaper, then spray the whole sculpture with matt black spray paint.

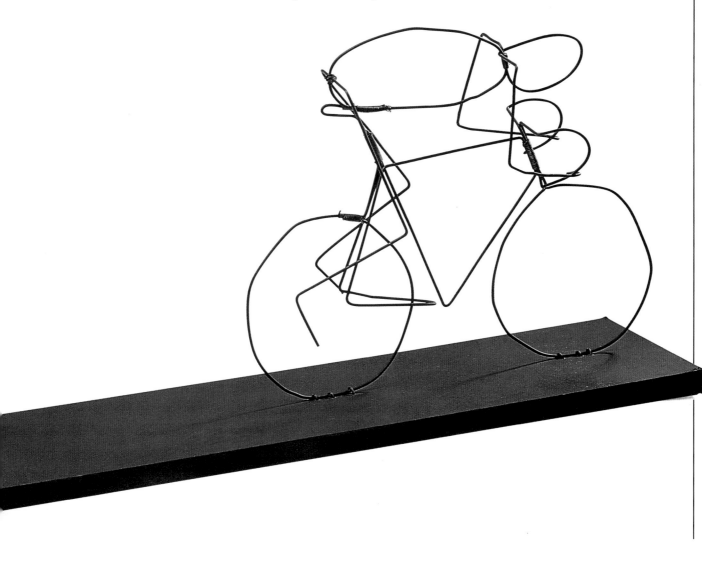

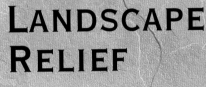

LANDSCAPE RELIEF

THIS PROJECT, LIKE "Fruit Relief" (see pp. 100–5), concentrates on the attractions of relief sculpture using a combination of construction and shaping (carving) techniques. The project focuses on the interplay between real and illusory space, important attributes of relief sculpture. A landscape vista illustrates a simple rule of perspective: that objects nearer to you appear bigger than those which are furthest away.

Photographs of landscapes are very useful because they are unchanging, allowing you to concentrate on identifying the receding elements and the way the eye perceives them. From the photographs, make drawings reducing the elements of the composition to a progression of hill forms that recede to a single point. By studying your chosen drawing you can establish the part of the sculpture which should be raised the most – the points which are nearest; and which should be the lowest – *ie* the part of the landscape which is furthest away. It is this sculptural device that draws the eye into the work.

Using aluminium foil with polystyrene tiles will help you to explore and exploit different surface textures, while the application of colour creates spatial effects and enhances perspectival space. Polystyrene tiles are very easy to shape with a small wire brush – one you would use for cleaning suede shoes is adequate.

▲ Sketches reduce the elements of the composition to a progression of hill forms that recede to a point.

Materials

MDF board 75 × 30 × 1 cm
(30 × 12 × ½ in)
2 hanging hooks
PVA glue
polystyrene tiles
aluminium foil
double-sided clear
adhesive tape
decorating filler
black acrylic paint

Equipment

pencil
paper
bradawl
paintbrush
tape measure
felt-tip pen
craft knife
ruler
scissors
old kitchen knife
filling knife
sandpaper
small wire brush
cloth

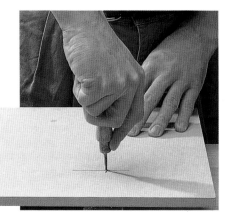

1 Make two holes with a bradawl on the back of the board. Each one should be 13 cm (5 in) in from the side and 7.5 cm (3 in) down from the top. Then screw a hanging hook into each hole.

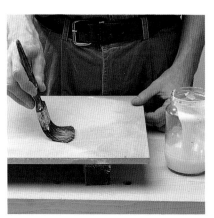

2 Turn the board over. Paint on two coats of diluted PVA glue, not forgetting the edges of the board. Allow the first coat to dry before recoating.

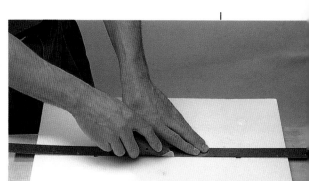

3 Because the polystyrene tiles are bigger than the board they need to be cut to size. Cut two polystyrene tiles, one to measure 45 × 30 cm (18 × 12 in), the other 30 × 30 cm (12 × 12 in).

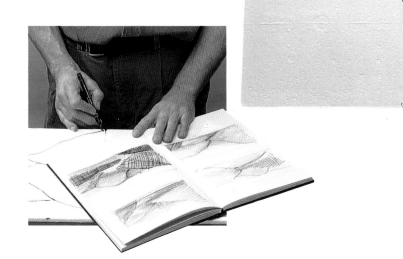

5 Even at this stage you appreciate the visual trickery involved; the shapes retreating backwards create a sense of perspective.

4 Refer to your landscape drawings. Draw the profile of the five hills onto the polystyrene.

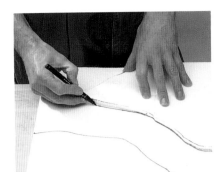

7 Use these five shapes as templates. One by one, place a shape on top of another tile. Draw around it and cut out the shape with the craft knife.

8 Starting with the smallest shape – that which is farthest away – you need one tile cutting; increase the number by one as the hills become nearer, until you reach shape Number 5 which needs five tile cuttings. ▼

6 Using a craft knife, cut along the drawn lines to create five separate shapes. At this stage, two of the shapes will be composed of two pieces of joined polystyrene. Treat each of these as a single shape when following step 7.

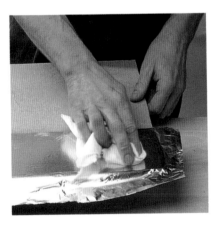

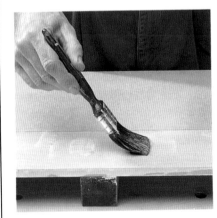

9 Draw a line parallel to and 10 cm (4 in) down from the top of the board. Paint a generous coat of PVA glue onto this top section of the board.

10 Place a piece of aluminium foil over the glue-painted section. When lowering it down onto the board, hold it as taut as possible. Gently lower it, keeping the edge lined up with the drawn line. Smooth the foil down with a cloth, working from the centre outwards.

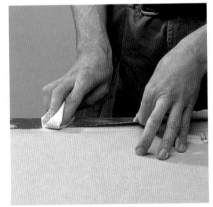

11 Turn the board over. Paint enough PVA on the board to take the overlap of the foil. Holding the foil taut, gently smooth it down onto the board with a cloth.

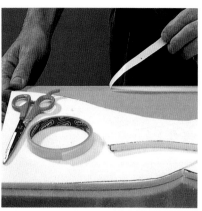

12 This band of foil effectively becomes the sky for the relief. The line created at the junction of the foil and the board is the horizon line.

13 The first layer of shapes can now be stuck onto the board, using double-sided clear adhesive tape. Stick the tape onto the board, peel off the backing, then fix the polystyrene shape on top. Push it down firmly to ensure that it sticks to the tape.

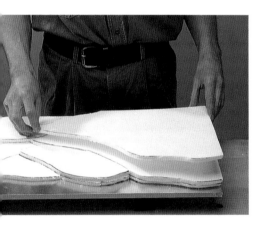

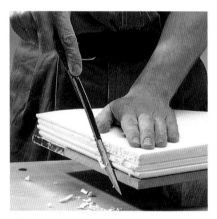

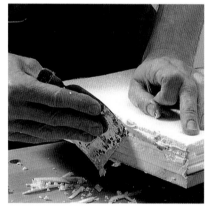

14 Use the same method to stick polystyrene to polystyrene, making sure that when bonding one identical shape to another you line them up and that they fit snugly on top of one another.

15 You will find that some overlaps are unavoidable along the edge. Trim these off with an old kitchen knife.

16 Use decorating filler along each side and along the bottom to fill in inconsistencies in the layers of polystyrene. When dry smooth it down with sandpaper.

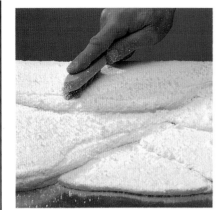

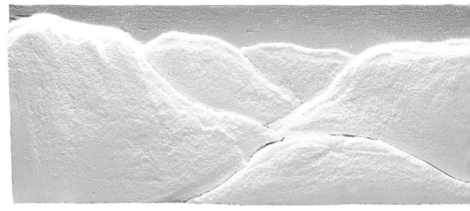

17 With a small wire brush, shape each of the areas of polystyrene into landscape forms. You will find that the polystyrene is very easy to shape with the brush.

18 At this stage you can see how effective the shaping of polystyrene has been, creating both real and illusory space. Notice also how the shaping has been carried from the sides into the centre.

19 Paint on a generous coat ▶ of glue onto the smallest shape. Place a piece of aluminium foil onto this and hold in place. Push it firmly down onto the surface and well into the edges.

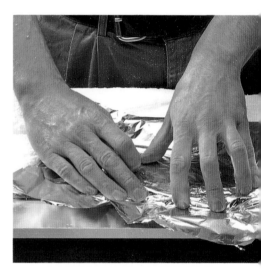

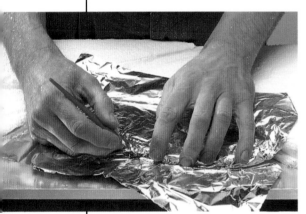

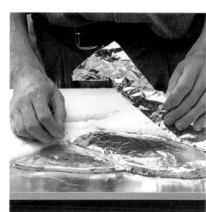

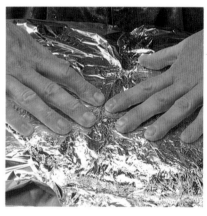

20 Using a sharp craft knife slowly and carefully cut away the excess foil. Be extra vigilant when doing this because the foil can tear very easily.

21 Continue this process over each of the shapes. Cut the excess carefully and lift it away. Notice that there is an overlap of the foil onto the adjoining polystyrene shape.

22 On one of the larger areas apply the foil as before but use both hands to push it together to produce an interesting texture.

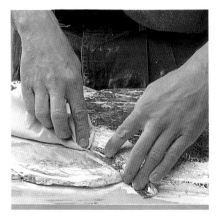 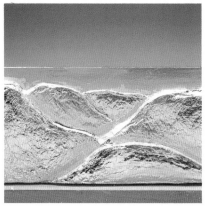 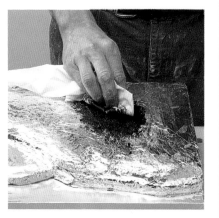

23 Where shapes join there may be gaps between the foil. If so, cut a long thin strip, brush glue into the crevice, add the strip of foil, then push it firmly down with a cloth.

24 The whole relief has now been covered in foil. You can see how it has faithfully adhered to the shaped undulations of the polystyrene underneath. The surface textures created by the foil also are very noticeable. Leave for 24 hours to allow the PVA to dry.

25 Using a cloth, rub some black acrylic paint onto the surface. Work it into the crevices well and into the textured surface of the polystyrene. Before the paint has dried, wipe most of it away, ensuring that the crevices retain the paint.

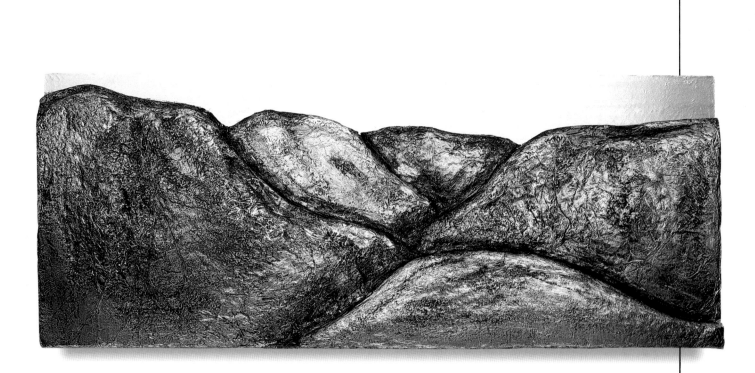

PORCUPINE

A pincushion and pins provide an opportunity to experiment with directions and relative heights before you begin banging in nails.

Nature presents many inspiring subjects for artists and sculptors. Among them are plants and animals covered in protective spikes – such as cacti, the horsechestnut, the hedgehog and the porcupine. In these last two examples, it is difficult to define the form concealed by the spikes but you are very much aware of the form of the closely packed spikes.

Although taking inspiration from nature, this project does not seek to reproduce a porcupine. Instead, it strives to achieve a marriage of the geometric and the organic. A block of wood supplies the geometric touch; this contrasts with a gentle flowing movement created by the undulating bank of nails. An important aim is to use the straightness of the nails in a way that creates apparent movement over the surface of the block.

This sense of geometry is further illustrated by the fact that an equal number of holes is drilled into each face of the block, each hole being equidistant from the other. Doing this also gives you valuable experience using an electric drill and hammer in a controlled way. The question of control is an important element of this project. It is not just a case of banging the nails in willy-nilly; you need to be aware of their relative heights to one another and the direction in which they are going. This is particularly important when you move from one surface to another. Banging the nails in at a diagonal angle and gradually altering the direction of each nail will produce an even flow around the block. At the same time the colouring of the nails provides an interesting contrast with the black-painted wood.

◄ Unlike a porcupine, the form of a cactus is still very obvious under its prickly exterior.

Materials

timber 10 × 10 × 30 cm
(4 × 4 × 12 in)
masking tape
black emulsion paint
7.5 cm (3 in) oval nails

Equipment

tape measure
ruler
pencil
electric drill
3 mm (⅛ in) drill bit
hammer
pliers
paintbrush
G-clamp

Health/Safety

clear goggles

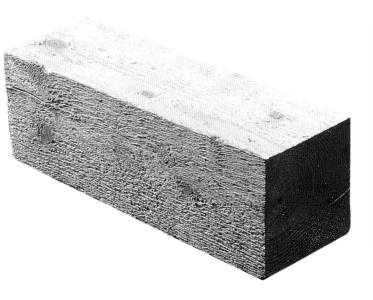

1 Start with a piece of 10 × 10 cm (4 × 4 in) softwood. This is a standard size, available from your local timber merchant. Get them to cut it to 30 cm (12 in) in length.

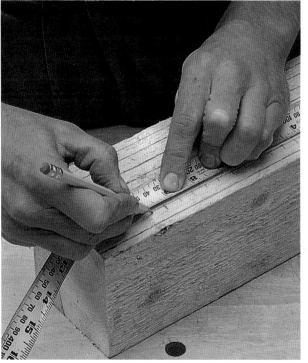

2 Make lines with your pencil every 1 cm (½ in) on the back and front edges along the length of the wood.

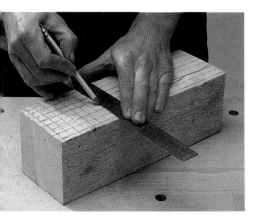

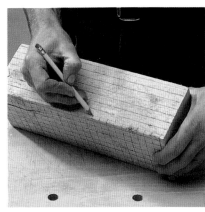

3 Start 5 mm (¼ in) along each of the corresponding short edges. Make marks with your pencil every 1 cm (½ in). With your ruler and pencil join the marks on the opposite edges with a straight line.

4 You now have a grid on one ◄ of the faces. Mark out and join up the two opposite short edges on the next face of the block. Use the grid already made on the previous face to mark the edge of this face. Use your ruler to mark out the opposite edges. Join these marks.

5 Draw a grid onto the two remaining long faces. Use the grid on these long faces as a guide to mark out the short ends and produce grids on both ends of the wood block. ▼

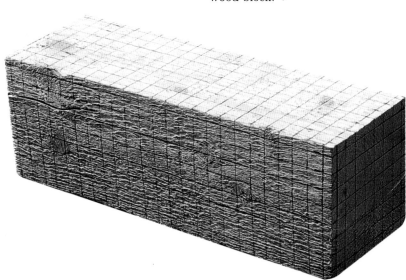

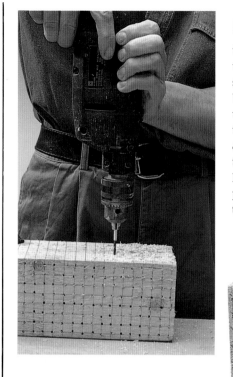

6 Where each of the lines ◀ intersect on the grid you need to drill a 2.5 cm (1 in) deep hole with a 3 mm (⅛ in) drill bit. Fix a strip of masking tape on the drill bit 2.5 cm (1 in) up from its tip – this will act as a depth indicator. Clamp the block to your work surface with a G-clamp. When drilling on the two end faces, drill in horizontally, keeping the block clamped in position with the end face pointing toward you.

7 Drill the requisite holes on all six surfaces of the wood block. It is very time-consuming, and so probably repays drilling one face at a time, allowing a break before starting another face. ▼

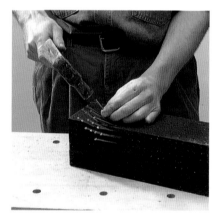

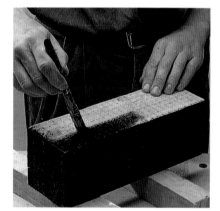

8 Paint the block with black emulsion paint. Wait until the top three surfaces are dry before turning it over to paint the underside. Apply two coats of paint in order to obtain density of colour.

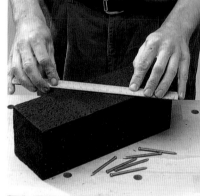

9 Place your ruler diagonally along one of the faces of the block, so that it is in line with a series of holes. Move the ruler up and down the face to find a diagonal line that will move across one face to another.

10 Hammer in your 5 cm (2 in) oval nails at an angle, establishing an initial grouping that crosses from one face to another.

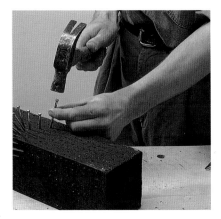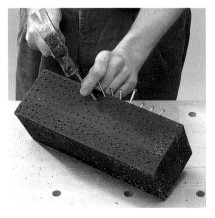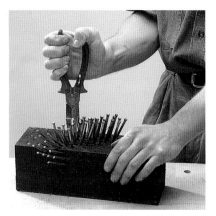

11 Continue banging in the nails on a diagonal line along this face, at the same time changing the angle at which the nails are banged in order to create a feeling of movement around the surface.

12 Continue to establish a line of nails travelling over and around the block.

13 Try to keep the angle at which the nails are banged in changing gently in relation to one another. Use pliers to make adjustments.

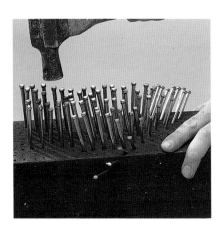

14 Hammer in a clutch of 7.5 cm (3 in) oval nails along the centre of one of the faces, keeping the heads vertical and at the same height. Now hammer a group of nails hard and consistently. Your intention is to create an indentation that rises up smoothly, joining with the flow of nails moving around the block.

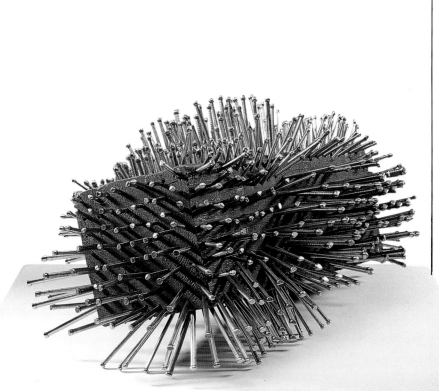

DRAPERY AND CHAIR

I F YOU LOOK at figurative sculpture, from antique times to the present day, you can see how often drapery forms part of the composition. When it works best, drapery does not totally obscure or camouflage the sculpted forms but encourages the eye to fully explore them. In this project you will be investigating how folds of drapery can be moulded to search out and enhance a sculpture.

Compose a still life by draping a length of cloth over a chair. This will be the model for your sculpture. Note that there is an interesting contrast between the geometric construction of the chair and the soft sinuous folds of the drapery.

Wax is the ideal material for your purpose because you will be able to exploit this contrast. Making use of the proper material for the subject you want to tackle is an important facet of sculpture, and of this project in particular. Here you will be working with wax that has been cast into slabs – a sculptural technique. Wax is available in various grades, according to its hardness and the proposed use. Casting wax is used in this project because it is hard and thus suitable for assuming the chair's shape but at the same time is extremely flexible. When placed in hot water, it is easily bent and shaped, but once cool becomes hard and firm and will keep its shape, unless exposed to heat again.

This project makes use of another rich aspect of sculpture – its spatial possibilities. The completed wax sculpture is placed on a base. This itself defines an area of space within which the sculpture exists, as in "Racing Cyclist" (see pp. 76–9). But there also exists an enclosed space under the chair which is exploited as part of the overall composition by using drapery to link it to the chair itself, as well as the base.

▼ Start by looking at hanging coats, piles of clothes, curtains, drapes and other textiles. Draw some of these to get an understanding of how the cloth responds to gravity, and to forms beneath it.

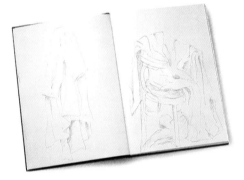

Materials

washing-up liquid
block of casting wax

Equipment

sheet of glass
sponge
**strips of wood approx 3 mm
(⅛ in) thick**
old kitchen knife
camping gas stove
saucepan
stirrer
ruler
craft knife
small screwdriver
container for hot water

Health/Safety

canvas gloves

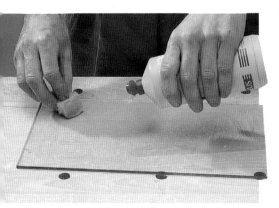

1 Use a sponge to rub some washing-up liquid onto a sheet of glass. This will stop the wax sticking to it after it has been poured and set.

2 Cut four strips of wood, each about 3mm (⅛in) thick, to fit the four sides of the glass. Coat each strip with washing-up liquid, then place them on top of and along the edges of the glass. Make sure that you position them securely and that the ends butt up to one another so as not to have any gaps showing.

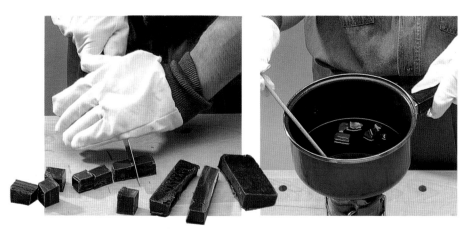

3 You will find that the block of wax is somewhat hard. Heat the blade of your knife gently in the flame of the gas burner. It will facilitate easy cutting of the block into cubes. Make sure that you wear gloves as the blade of the knife will be hot.

4 Put the cubes of wax into the saucepan and place on the gas burner. Keep your gloves on and stir continuously. The wax will quickly melt – be careful to avoid being splashed by hot wax.

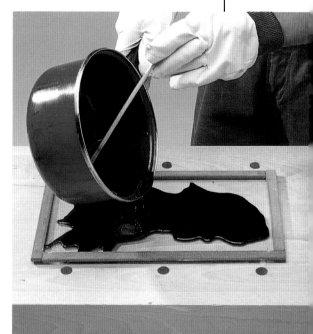

5 Pour the melted wax slowly and evenly onto the glass, ensuring that it covers the whole area up to the level of the frame. Hold the saucepan as close as possible to the glass when pouring. If you pour quickly and/or from a height the wax will splash and could also dislodge the frame.

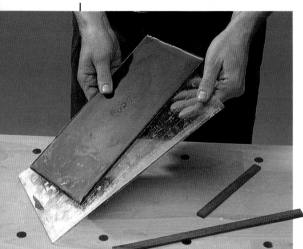

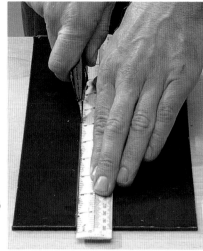

6 Depending on the surrounding temperature the slab of wax will have cooled and set hard after about 30 minutes. Remove the wooden frame and gently slide the slab of wax off the glass. You will need to make three such slabs for this sculpture.

7 From one slab cut a piece 30 × 10cm (12 × 4in), by making two marks at the top and bottom of the slab, 5cm (2in) in from one of the sides. Position a ruler along the marks and cut through the wax with the craft knife.

8 Cut the larger of the two pieces again to produce a piece 20 × 10cm (8 × 4in) and one 10 × 10cm (4 × 4in). From the remainder of the slab cut two pieces 10 × 2.5cm (4 × 1in). All these pieces will be used in constructing the chair.

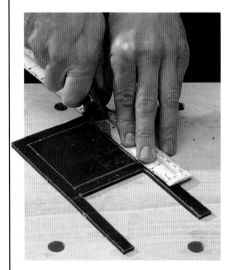

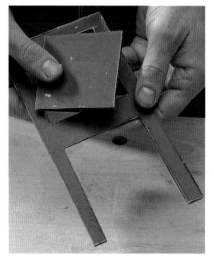

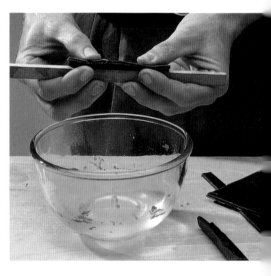

9 From the bottom of the 20 × 10cm (8 × 4in) slab cut away a section measuring 9 × 7.5cm (3½ × 3in), leaving two legs each about 1cm (½in) wide. Measuring 1cm (½in) down from the top, cut out another almost square piece, 9 × 7.5cm (3½ × 3in).

10 Gently push this section out of the wax. You now have the back section of the chair.

11 Place the two 10 × 2.5cm (4 × 1in) strips, one at a time, in hot water. The wax will quickly become malleable. Using a strip of wood, bend the wax down at right angles along it to create the two front legs of the chair.

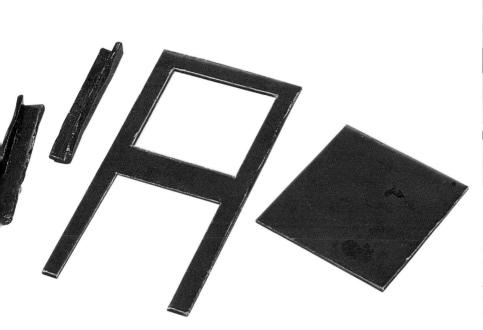

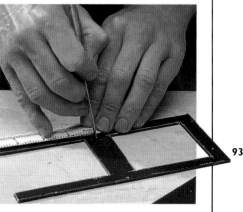

13 Pick up the back section. Measuring from the bottom of each leg, make a mark 10cm (4in) up on the horizontal band that joins the two legs. Here the seat section will be joined at right angles to the back.

12 You now have four parts of the chair – back with legs, two front legs, and the seat. They can now be joined together to make the chair.

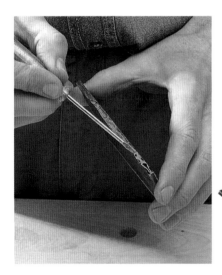

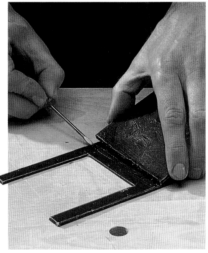

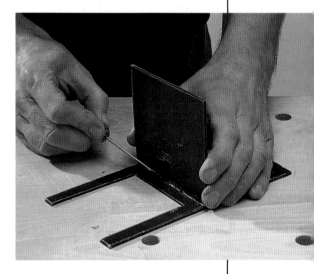

14 The seat and back are welded together with the hot tip of a screwdriver by melting the two pieces at their point of contact and then quickly joining them so that the molten wax on each part flows together. Once cool, the wax becomes one. This is not a difficult technique and will not take long to learn.

15 To join the seat to the chair, heat the tip of the screwdriver in the flame of the burner and run the hot screwdriver along the marked line on the horizontal of the chair back. Then apply the hot screwdriver to the edge of the seat. Quickly join the two parts together, making sure that the chair seat is at right angles to the back.

16 Once in position, further strengthen the weld by running the hot screwdriver along the join. This further melds together the wax of the seat and back.

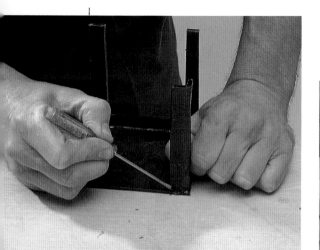

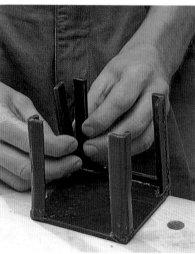

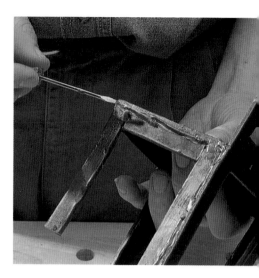

17 With the chair upside down, and the back hanging down the front of the bench, join on the two front legs, using the same technique.

18 Weld an extra strip onto the two back legs, so that their shape corresponds with the two front legs.

19 Finally, add three 1cm (½in) strips of wax to the underside of the seat, to give the impression of a more solid chair.

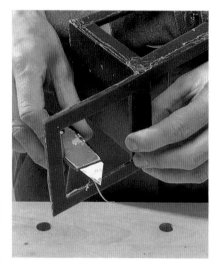

20 Any unsightly lumps of wax can be trimmed off with a craft knife.

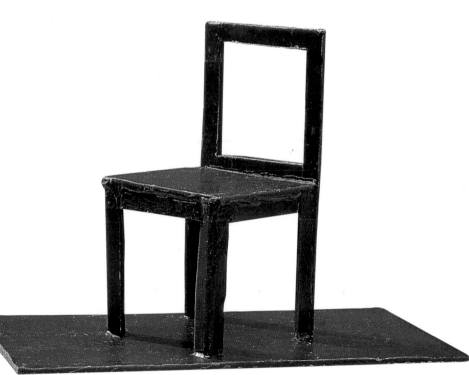

21 Use another cast slab as the base for the sculpture. Position the chair and fix into place by melting the legs onto the base.

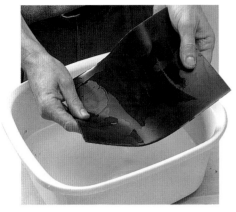 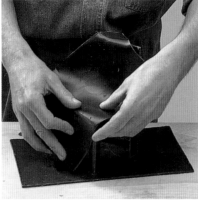 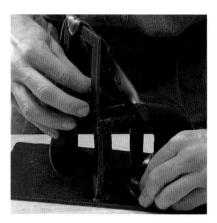

22 A slab of wax is now going to be draped over the chair. To get the slab malleable enough, place it in a container of hot water. Move it around in the water until it is really soft and flexible.

23 Before the wax has a chance to cool, drape it over the chair. Create the bends and folds that you observed while drawing this situation from life.

24 Use a smaller piece of wax as drapery to investigate the space underneath the chair, and the space defined by the base.

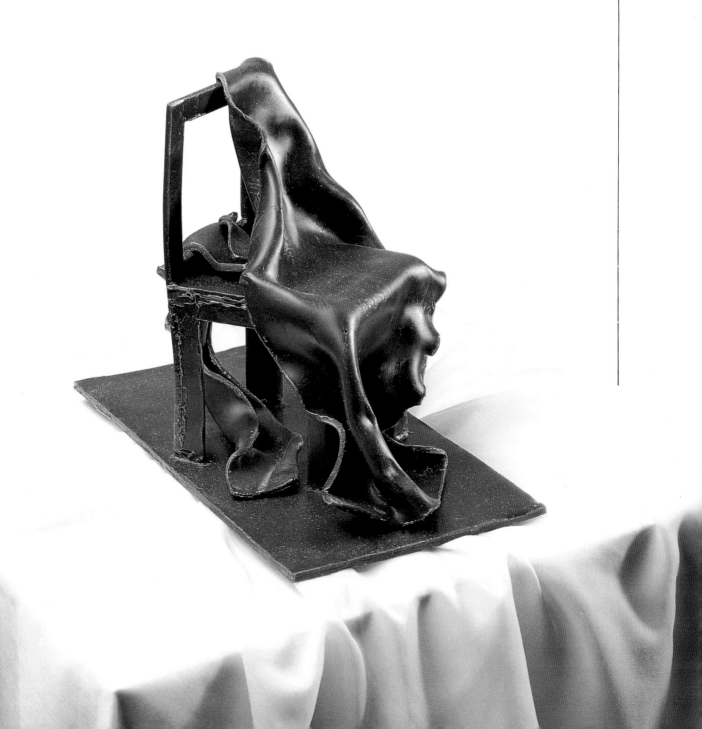

COMPOSITIONAL DEVICES

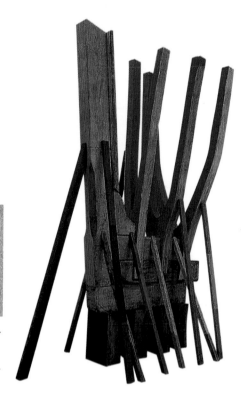

COMMUNICATION IN any spoken or written language does not require all of its vocabulary to be used. The same applies to sculpture: a good sculpture uses only what is necessary to communicate what the sculptor intended. The language of sculpture therefore needs to be learnt, and as much of this is "hands on" – such as the use of the different techniques and materials – it can be learnt while working practically.

One vital part of the language is composition. Compositional devices exist to help the sculptor. These are nothing to do with enabling a sculpture to exist physically, but are purely visual devices which are necessary to complete the composition of the sculpture. Indeed, the sculpture would be incomplete without them. The sculptures in this section all make use of such a visual device. There are no hard and fast rules for when or how to use such devices and invariably they are deemed to be necessary during the process of making a sculpture and so are difficult to preplan.

Sometimes when looking at a piece of sculpture we do not realize that visual devices are there because they are so taken for granted, but without them the work would suffer greatly – or even fail –

as a piece of sculpture. As with any language the language of sculpture needs to be learnt, so try to identify such devices when looking at sculpture. Look, learn and remember what they are and appreciate their importance – you never know when you might need to make use of this knowledge.

▲ **Robert Callender**
NEW BEGINNINGS

This sculpture is made from reinforced cardboard which has been painted to give the illusion that it is wood. The sculpture has a strong structural bias due to the various elements giving the impression that they are a much heavier material than in reality. They therefore seem dependent on each other for support.
441 × 274 × 152 cm
(173½ × 108 × 60 in)

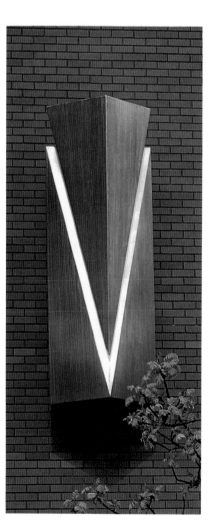

◀ **Michael Marriott**
SPLIT FORM NO. 4

By splitting this geometric form diagonally and positioning the two parts to give the impression of a slippage a dynamic abstract sculpture has been created using basic geometry. It is sited on the side of a building and blends in very well with the geometric nature of present-day architecture.
3 m (1 yd) high

▲ Rosemarie McGoldrick
FITTING DESCRIPTION

Instead of using a traditional composite relief format, each of the forms is separate and has been placed on the wall in a horizontal configuration reminiscent of decoration to be found on the exterior and interior of buildings. The strong horizontal line that runs across the top of the sculpture visually holds the disparate elements together.
1.5 × 6.7 m (5 × 22 ft)

▶ Guy Thomas
HEART OF THE VILLAGE

This sculpture is made from forged steel. It makes use of an enclosed space which is revealed by the surrounding form which rhythmically moves around it, allowing the eye to explore the forms and spaces contained in the sculpture.
63.5 × 23 × 20 cm
(25 × 9 × 8 in)

▲ Robert Neilson
BLAIM

The base of this sculpture plays an important role by defining a space within which the arc-shaped segments can be butted up against one another to create a circle. This is further enhanced compositionally by the use of tyre treads.
30.5 × 366 × 366 cm
(12 × 144 × 144 in)

▶ Laura White
ESCAPE

Carved in Ancaster Harwhite limestone, the composition of this sculpture relies on the creation of a continuous movement that runs through it. The movement is interrupted by the vertical indentation.
38 × 25 × 23 cm (15 × 10 × 9 in)

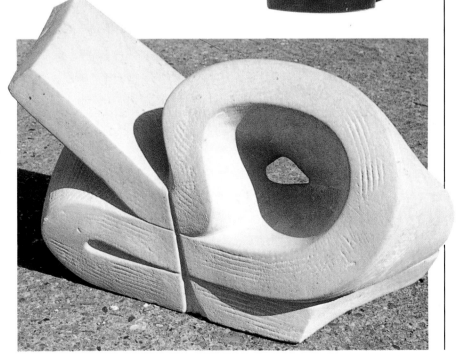

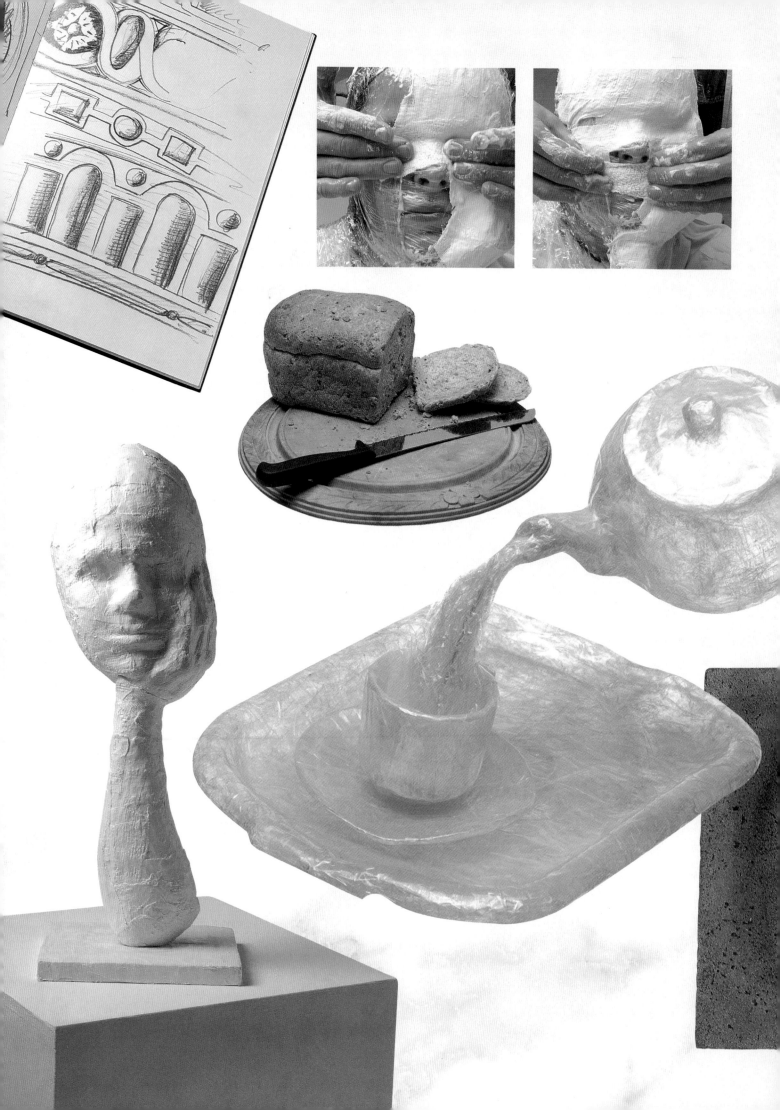

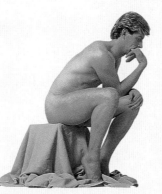
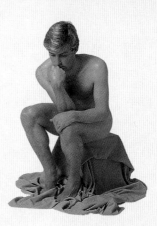

4

CASTING

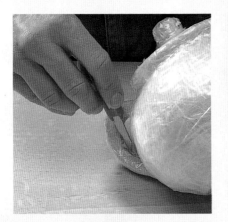

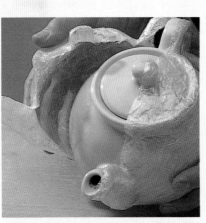

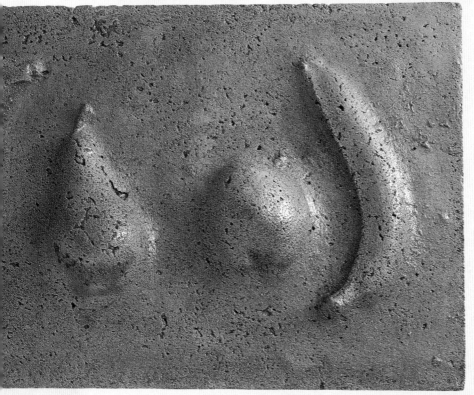

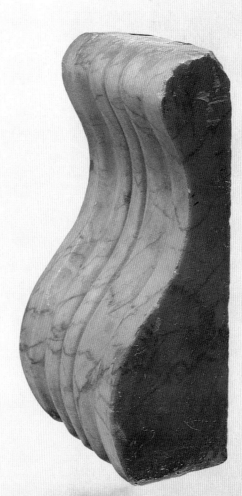

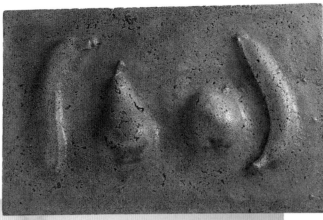

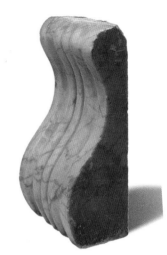

FRUIT RELIEF

Making a mould and producing a cast from this mould are both basic sculpting processes. They come into their own when a sculpture made in a soft material, such as clay, is to be reproduced – *ie* cast – in a more permanent and durable material. Bronze is the traditional option. A mould gives a negative impression of the original form, the positive. The complexity of the forms contained in the original sculpture will be difficult to mould, consequently this should only be attempted once you have a better understanding of the techniques involved. This project introduces you to the press-mould technique – the simplest way to make a mould – and utilizes a straightforward casting technique.

The casting material is a sand and cement mix, available in ready-mixed bags. All you have to do is add water and mix. The impressions of the fruit are made in a bed of clay, available from an art material supplier. This can be reused for press-moulds or for modelling. Although fruit has been chosen, any firm item can be used, as long as it can be easily disengaged from the clay. Remember when planning your composition that what reads left to right in the clay impression will read right to left in the cement cast.

Because the cast is being made in cement, the sculpture could go in the garden, be fixed to a building or embedded in a brick wall.

▲ Look at the wide variety of architectural decoration on buildings, both inside and out. Museums are also useful sources of decorative detail.

Materials

sawn timber 7.5 × 5 cm (3 × 2 in); two at 30 cm (12 in), two at 45 cm (18 in)
4 strips of plywood, approx 7.5 × 3.5 cm (3 × 1½ in)
1.5 cm (¾ in) panel pins
pear
apple
two bananas
chicken wire
5 kg (11 lb) pack ready-mixed sand and cement

Equipment

saw
vegetable oil
polythene
set square
small hammer
rolling pin
screwdriver
wire cutters
rag
bucket
timber 5 × 5 × 30 cm (2 × 2 × 12 in)

Health/Safety

rubber gloves
cotton gloves

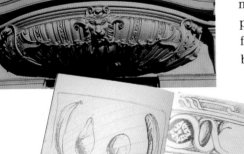

▲ Make drawings of architectural details that please you, either from the actual building itself or from photographs in books.

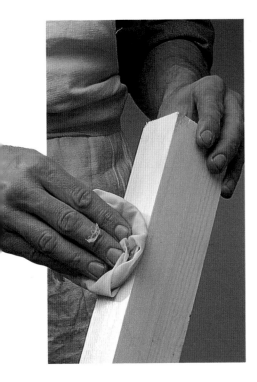

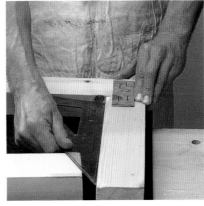

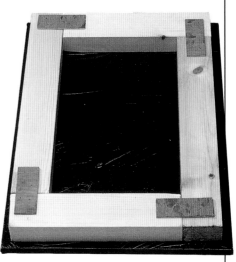

3 On each of the corners fix plywood pieces with panel pins to hold the angles firm. The jig is now ready for use. ▼

2 With the four pieces of timber, create a rectangular jig, 5 cm (2 in) deep, on a polythene-covered modelling board. Use a set square to ensure the corners of the jig are at right angles.

1 After sawing two pieces of 7.5 × 5 cm (3 × 2 in) timber 30 cm (12 in) long, and two at 45 cm (18 in) long, thoroughly coat them in vegetable oil. This acts as a release agent and prevents the clay and cement from sticking to the wood.

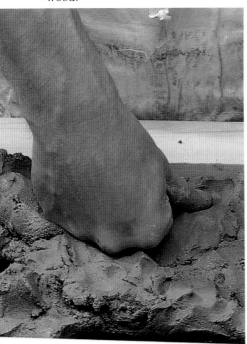

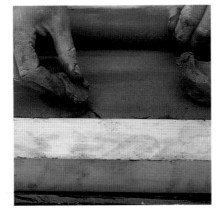

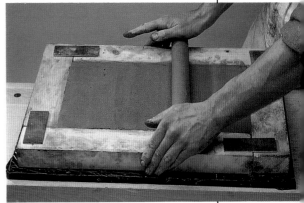

5 As the clay nears the top, use a rolling pin to create a flat and level surface. Any holes or gaps in the surface must be filled with well-packed clay.

6 Straddle the rolling pin over the clay so that each end of the pin is resting on the wooden sides. Roll the pin back and forth until the clay is smooth, flat and even with the surround.

4 Fill the interior of the jig with clay, pressing it well down into the jig. You need to pack the clay up to the top of the wooden sides – *ie* 5 cm (2 in) deep.

Safety

● **Wear rubber gloves when working with the cement mixture**
● **Wear cotton gloves when cutting the chicken wire to size**

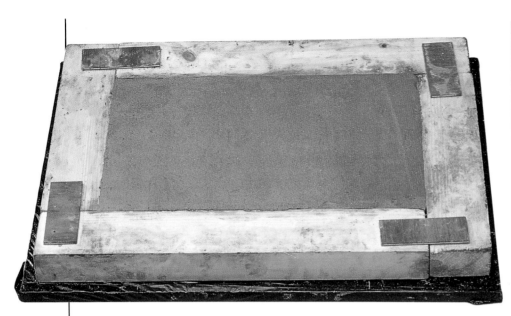

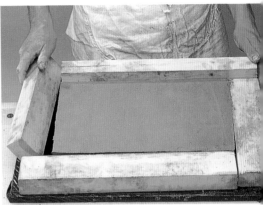

7 A suitable bed of clay has now been created. With a screwdriver gently prise away the pieces of plywood in each corner.

8 Turn the pieces of wood comprising the jig around, so that each rests on its 5 cm (2 in) side. This creates a 10 cm (4 in)-high box that is tight against the side of the clay. Turning the wood around creates an overlap, and the wood must be staggered to reform the box around the bed of clay. Reuse the plywood strips and panel pins, fixing them at each corner to steady the box.

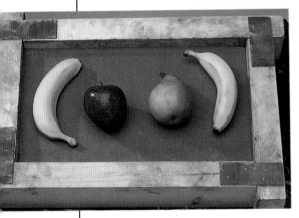

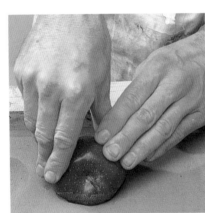

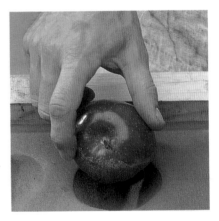

9 The reconstituted box in position. The arrangement of the fruit makes a pleasing composition, bearing in mind that the right hand banana will be on the left in the resultant cast.

10 Firmly press each piece of fruit into the clay, pushing it down as far as you are able while making sure that it can be easily removed.

11 Gently remove the apple to reveal a concave impression of it. The banana is a soft fruit, so when you are pressing down do not use too much force since it is easy to squash.

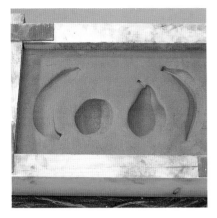

12 You have now obtained impressions of four fruits. Note how you obtained the stalk of the pear, but not of the apple. This is because it would have meant pushing the apple in too far, making its removal difficult. This could have spoiled the entire mould.

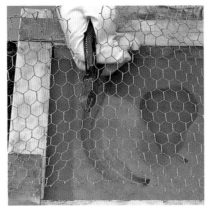

13 Since chicken wire will be used at a later stage, this is a good point to cut it. Lay some on top of the clay bed and trim it so that it is about 1 cm (½ in) in from the wood all the way around.

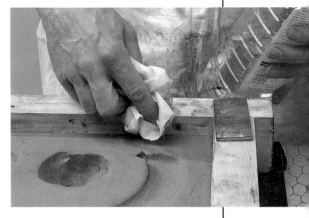

14 Use vegetable oil to recoat those surfaces of the wood that will come into contact with the cement.

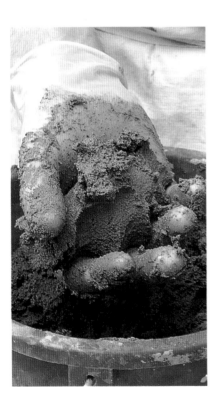

15 Pour the ready-mixed sand and cement into a bucket. Add water and mix well in. The mix must reach the consistency of cottage cheese: not too runny and not too dry.

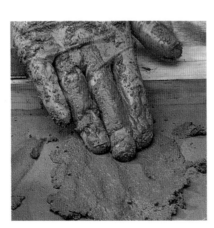

16 Take a small clod of the mix and pat it down into the first impression. Pat it well to eliminate air bubbles and ensure that the cement reaches all the nooks and crannies of the clay mould.

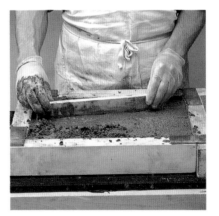

17 After filling all four impressions, continue filling the jig with cement, covering the surface of the clay mould, until it is 1 cm (½ in) from the top of the wood. Use another piece of wood to tamp (pat) down the cement, creating a level surface. As you tamp down, water will rise to the surface of the cement.

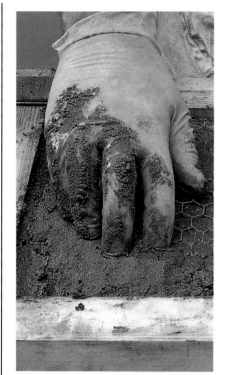

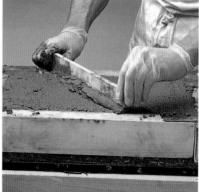

18 Take the piece of chicken wire and firmly embed it in the cement. Then cover the wire with more cement, up to the level of the wood.

19 Use the sides of the jig as a guide to tamp down and level off the surface of the cement.

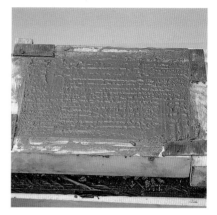

20 The cast is now complete. Put aside to allow the cement to dry – 48 hours is sufficient.

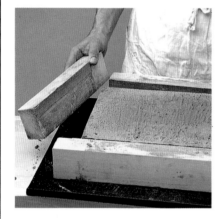

21 When the cement is dry, remove the strips of plywood with a screwdriver. Take away the wooden sides of the mould, being careful not to damage the edges of the cast.

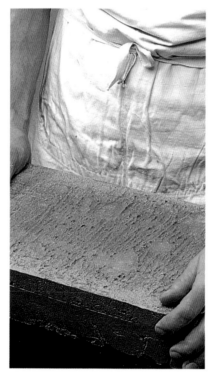

22 Now the mould and cast must be turned over. Gently slide the block toward you until most of it is off the board. You can now up-end it and carefully turn it over. Lower it gently so that the clay bed is now on top.

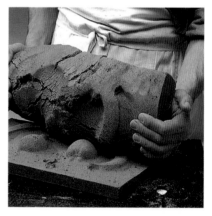

23 Take the corners of the clay and peel it back slowly to reveal the cement cast.

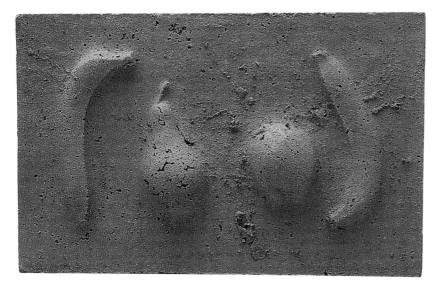

24 Bits of clay must be cleaned off the cement cast, which will still be wet and green in colour. There are also a few cavities on the surface of the cast; these have been caused by air being trapped between the cement and the clay, giving the cement an interesting stone-like quality.

25 Leave the cement cast to dry completely. This will depend on the surrounding humidity and temperature, but if kept indoors it should take about a week. When the relief is thoroughly dry, varnish the surface. This darkens the relief, accentuating the modulations and attractive imperfections of the surface.

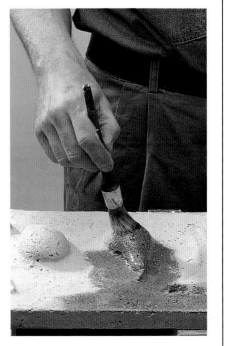

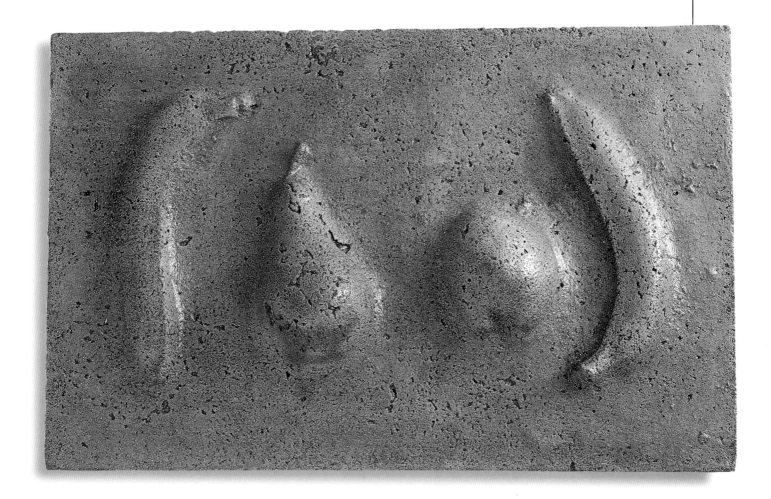

Materials

plaster-impregnated bandage
(mod roc)
clingfilm
MDF 20 × 20 × 2 cm
(8 × 8 × ¾ in)
45 cm (18 in) dowelling
PVA glue

Equipment

pencil
ruler
sketch pad
newspaper
scissors
bowl of water
G-clamp
13 mm (½ in) zip bit
electric drill
paintbrush

Health/Safety

barrier cream

HEAD ON HAND

T RADITIONALLY, CASTING REQUIRES a mould which contains a negative impression of the original subject. This was the case in "Fruit Relief" (see pp. 100–5). In the present project, you will use a more modern technique where a positive form is used to produce another positive form. This is known as direct casting. Here a plaster-impregnated bandage is used to take a cast from parts of a figure. The purpose is to achieve a traditional figurative sculpture in a traditional material – plaster.

Decide what body part or parts can be used to produce an interesting sculptural form. In this case I decided that the face, resting on a hand and supported by the vertical lines of the lower arm, provided an interesting sculptural composition. Explore the possibilities in your sketchbook. When making your drawings, remember that you are not trying to capture a facial likeness, but rather finding an interesting sculptural configuration of these two parts.

When actually working on the casting itself, there are important technical considerations to be borne in mind. Unlike the tea set on pp. 112–17, it is not possible to totally encase the subject in the plaster bandage; the chosen body part needs to be able to slip easily out of the cast. The casting process must be completed quickly. The sculpture in this project took 15 minutes, from the initial preparations to the removal of the cast. So before you start, familiarize yourself with the material and the technique. It might be an idea to act as your own first model, using your arm or leg. Taking a cast is not the end of the story. Presenting it for view is just as important. The life cast is fixed to the dowelling so that the sculpture gives the illusion that it is resting on the tip of its elbow.

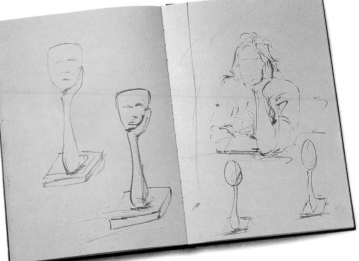

▲ First decide on a pose and then concentrate on the parts of the body to be used. Explore the possibilities in your sketchbook.

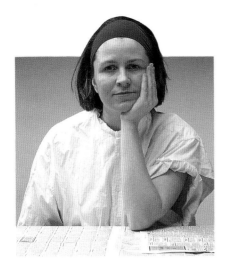

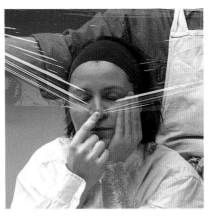

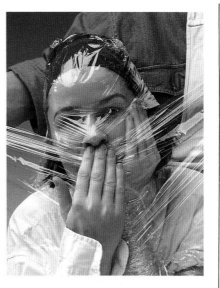

1 Using scissors, cut the bandage into several strips measuring 7.5 × 2.5 cm (3 × 1 in). It is better to have too much than not enough. Ensure that your model is positioned comfortably and is able to sustain that position. Here the model wears an old shirt to protect her clothes, while her hair is tied back leaving the relevant body areas exposed. The work surface has been protected with newspaper.

2 Use cling film to act as a barrier to prevent the plaster sticking to the body. Cover the arm and then cover the face MAKING SURE THAT THE NOSTRILS ARE LEFT UNCOVERED TO ALLOW THE MODEL TO BREATHE. Wrap the top half of the head first, getting the model to hold the cling film on the tip of her nose. Wrap it round the head and overlap it at the back so that it stays in place.

3 Next wrap the lower half of the head and face. Again ask the model to hold the cling film underneath her nostrils. Wrap the cling film around the head and overlap it at the back.

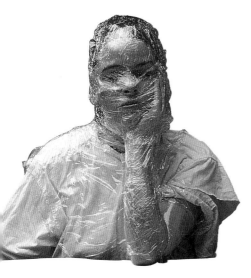

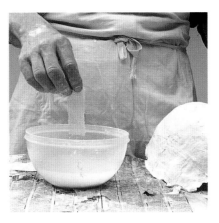

4 All exposed parts of the body have now been covered with cling film except for the nostrils. It is important to make sure that the model is comfortable. Emphasize that the model should alert you the moment there is any discomfort. If there is, abandon the operation straight away and remove everything from the model as quickly as possible.

5 To activate the bandage immerse in water. Lift it out immediately, keeping it flat and ensuring it does not wrinkle. Allow any excess water to drip off. You now only have about 3–4 minutes to work with it, so speed and efficiency are at a premium. This is also why it is important to pre-cut the bandage.

Safety

- **Use cling film on the model to prevent the plaster sticking to the body. However, make absolutely sure that the model's nostrils are left uncovered**
- **Do not wrap the plaster bandage too far around the body as this will prevent the plaster cast from being lifted cleanly and quickly from the body**
- **If at any time the model needs to be released from the cast, do so at once – don't worry about saving the cast**
- **Work quickly, since it starts to get uncom-fortable under the plaster as it sets**
- **Barrier cream will protect your hands**

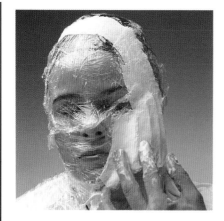

6 Starting from the top, lay the bandage down flat on the head, ensuring that it stays in place. Overlap another piece and work your way down the side of the head and over the hand, holding the bandage in place until it is just starting to set. When laying the bandage over specific areas, press it firmly so it is able to mould itself to that particular feature. If necessary, hold it in place until the bandage starts to set.

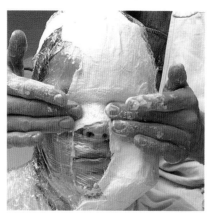

7 Continually working from the top to the bottom, move onto the face. Watch that the nostrils are kept clear, and at all times check with the model that everything is all right. When wrapping the eyes, push and hold the bandage in as far as is comfortable for the model.

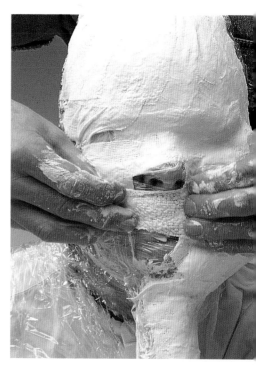

8 Do the same on the area under the nostrils and the lips.

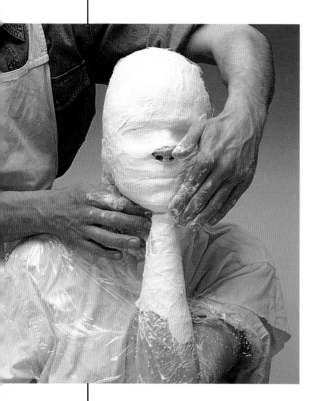

9 Continue around the side of the face and along the arm. When laying the bandage under the chin hold it in place. Do not carry the bandage too far under the chin, to avoid trapping the model in the cast.

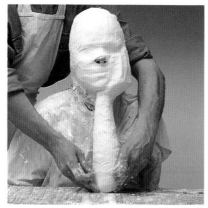

10 Now the bandage is in place on the upper arm. Continue laying on the bandage on the arm down to the elbow. Carry the bandage around the arm just enough to ensure that the model is able to release herself from the cast. Three layers of plaster bandage are sufficient.

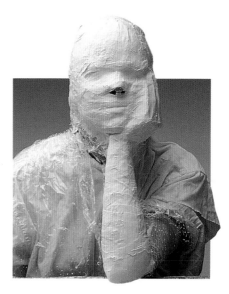

11 The task is now done. You can now appreciate how efficiently the bandage picks up detail. By now the model will have begun to feel uncomfortable beneath the plaster bandage.

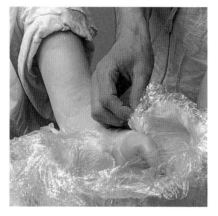

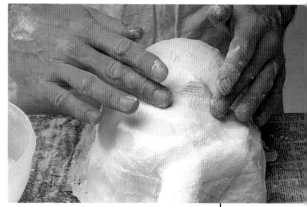

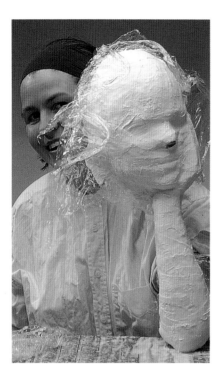

12 Quickly unwrap the cling film from the back of the model's head. By wiggling her head, the model should be able to release herself from the cast.

13 Now lower the arm onto the table, unwrap the cling film and release the arm from the cast.

14 Lay the cast face up on your work surface. Place a strip of bandage across the nostril gap.

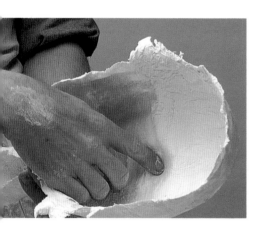

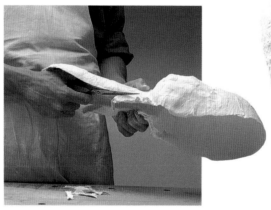

15 Quickly turn the head cast over and gently push the tip of the nostril out, holding your finger in place until that strip of bandage has set. Lay more bandage over this inside the cast to strengthen the nostril. Add another full layer of bandage over the whole back of the cast to strengthen it.

16 Trim off the surplus bandage with scissors from around the edges of the cast.

17 By trimming the edges ▶ you give the cast a very crisp profile emphasizing the clean moulding of the hand and facial features.

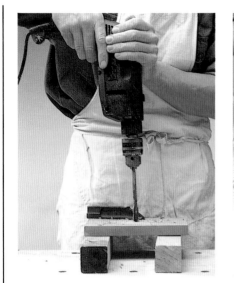

18 Drill a 1.5 cm (¾ in) hole into the centre of a 20 × 20 × 1.5 cm (8 × 8 × ¾ in) baseboard, which is clamped to your work surface. Use PVA glue to fix a 45 cm (18 in) length of dowelling into it.

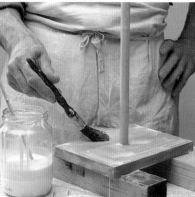

19 When the glue on the dowelling has set, coat the whole of the base with diluted glue. This seals the surface. Then lay over strips of plaster-impregnated bandage.

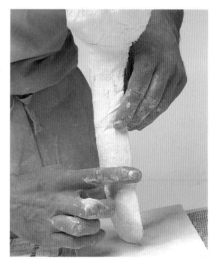

20 The base has now been covered with plaster bandage. This will act to blend the base and cast into a visual entity.

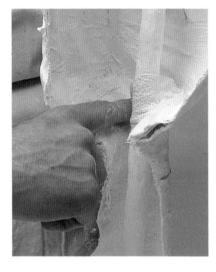

21 Hang the cast onto the vertical pole, ensuring that the elbow is just touching the base. The whole cast should be vertical. Working from the back, use plaster bandage to fix the pole to the cast at the top, neck and elbow points.

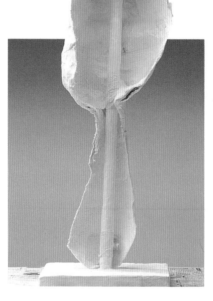

22 A back view of the mounting pole and the cast, showing the points at which they have been attached.

23 Now that the sculpture is fixed in place, tidy up the edges of the cast by wrapping short lengths of plaster bandage along them.

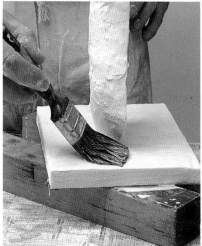

24 Finally, apply a coat of diluted PVA glue to the sculpture. This seals the surface of the sculpture and makes it less prone to become dirty and easier to clean.

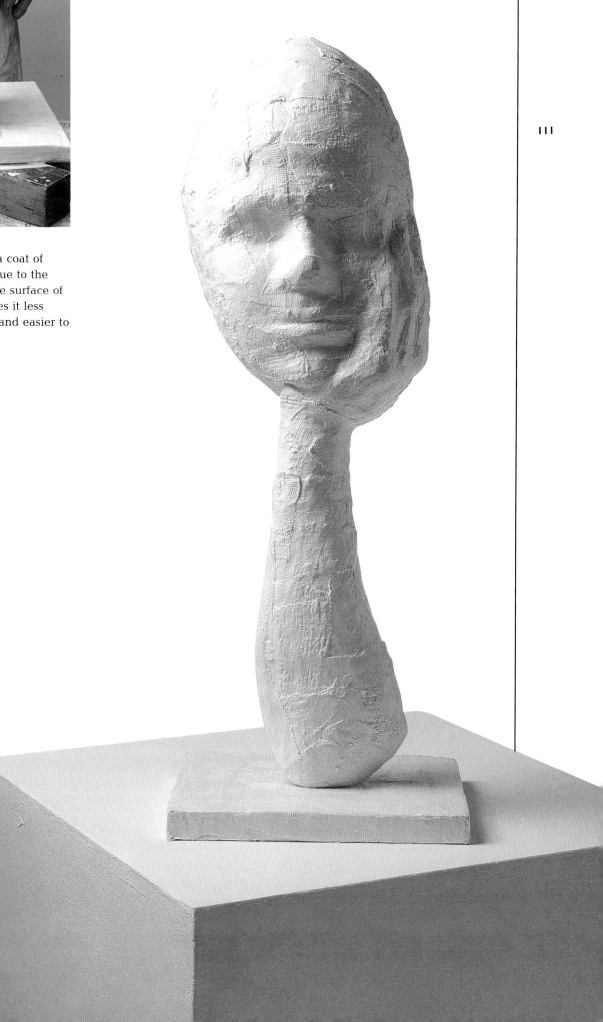

TEATIME

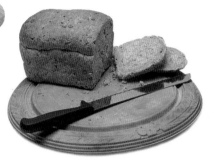

▲ This grouping of everyday objects needed for a familiar task is, in fact, a scene from a narrative and could be a suitable subject for a sculpture.

SOME SCULPTURE MAKES use of real objects or casts of objects, the sort of everyday things we see around us. Because we easily recognize such objects, and we know their uses and their relationships to other objects, it is possible to make a narrative sculpture, *ie* one that is telling a story. The narrative invoked by such a sculpture is totally dependent on the objects and the way they are positioned relative to one another.

To make a sculpture that reflects an everyday event in your life, think of situations that occur around you, especially where you have groupings of two or more objects needed for a familiar task. Make drawings of the grouping and of the individual objects. Then use your drawings to investigate interesting sculptural configurations of your chosen objects.

While the teapot, cup and saucer simply placed on a tray present a suggestive picture, its static nature defines it as a still life. But by lifting the teapot to pour tea into the cup, you have transformed the situation into a lively, narrative one. The illusion of the teapot caught in mid-pour creates a story invoking the passage of time. The illusion is technically achieved by the combined use of a wire support and a light clear adhesive tape cast. The wire support is fixed to the tray which, because of its large surface area, is able to act as a supporting base for the sculpture. The wire support goes up through the saucer and cup and is finally fixed inside the teapot.

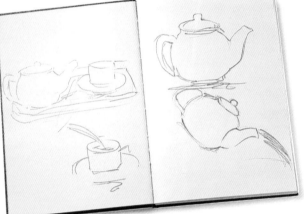

▲ Make drawings of the individual objects and experiment with potential groupings.

Materials

clear adhesive tape
teapot
cup
saucer
tray
clingfilm
wire coathanger

Equipment

small craft knife
pliers
bradawl

◀ If you look at your surroundings creatively, all manner of everyday objects can be formed into a narrative group.

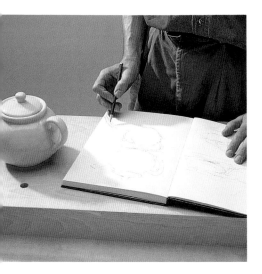

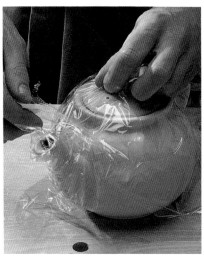

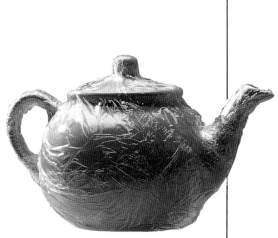

1 Display your chosen objects around you. If using the teaset, make drawings of its components. Develop the drawings into the proposed sculptural situation, in this case a teapot pouring into a cup.

2 Cover the teapot completely with cling film. This prevents the clear adhesive tape from sticking to it.

3 Check that the cling film has been wound tightly around the handle, spout and lid of the teapot. The cling film must be tight against the surface of the object.

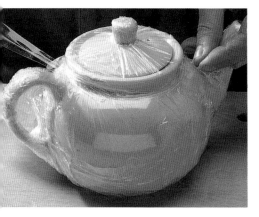

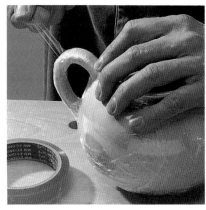

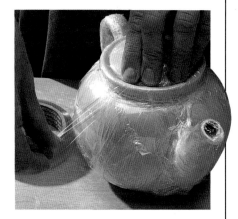

4 Starting from the top of the teapot, wrap the clear adhesive tape tightly around, ensuring that the tape closely follows the form. Use shorter lengths of tape when wrapping the lid.

5 The handle is a bit more tricky. Again, use short lengths of tape. Really pull it tightly when you wrap it around.

6 Build up the layers of tape on the main body of the teapot. Make sure that you push the tape into the crevice around the top. Don't stretch the tape over these areas and so miss details.

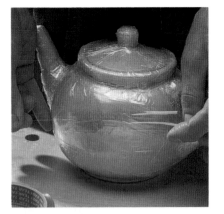

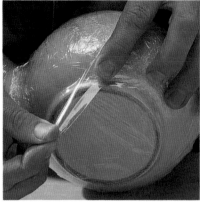

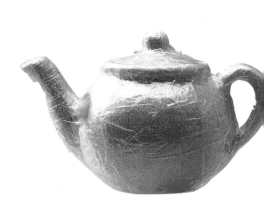

7 When building up the layers of tape, alternate the direction in which you apply it. Here it is laid on horizontally over vertical strips. This technique is easier to maintain on the main body of the teapot.

8 Don't forget the underside of the pot. Press the tape firmly against the surface to keep the impression of the rim underneath.

9 By now the clear adhesive tape has been built up thickly over the whole surface of the teapot. Because you are applying small lengths of tape at a time it is easy to lose count of the layers you are building up. Use your judgement as to when to stop. The tape "mummy" must look increasingly opaque, and *feel* well-bound.

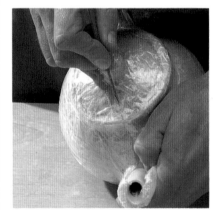

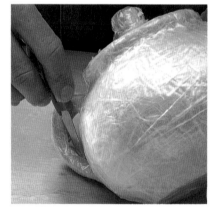

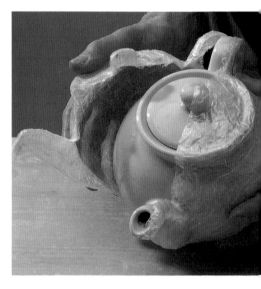

10 To remove the teapot from the tape use a craft knife to make an incision along its centre from the tip of the spout. Proceed to cut along the centre of the teapot, taking care with the sharp blade.

11 The interior of the handle will be tricky, as you can only get the knife in at an angle. Cut the tape as best you can; though it isn't a straight line, this can be rectified later.

12 With the tape cut all the way around, you can pull one half of the cast away from the teapot. Then remove the other side.

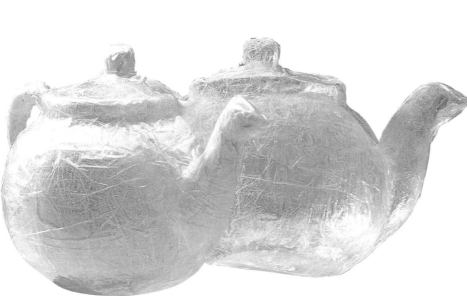

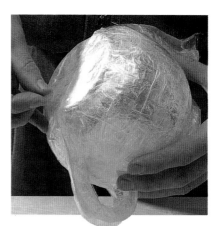

14 Hold the two halves in place with three bits of tape. Then securely tape them together, leaving the spout unfixed for the time being. It will be joined together at a later stage.

13 The clear tape should have been built up to a sufficient thickness to allow both halves to stand free and support themselves. Note how the tape replicates the forms of the object perfectly.

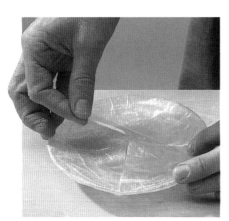

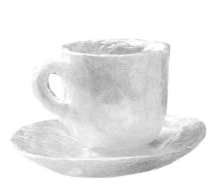

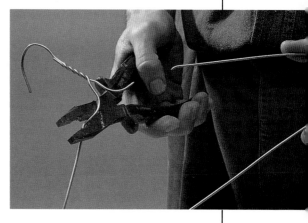

15 Cover the cup, saucer and tray in cling film and tape in the same manner. The way that you cut the tape to release the object will be slightly different, but the principle is the same: *ie* make the minimum amount of cuts to allow for easy removal. Here the adhesive tape saucer cast is being rejoined, after being cut along the centre and into sections to facilitate removal of the saucer.

16 The completed casts of the cup and saucer. The tape on the cup was cut centrally all the way around the outside and inside of the cup. The interior of the handle again was a tricky area to cut, but any uneveness was corrected when the cast was joined together.

17 Make a support to raise the teapot in the air – a wire coathanger should be strong enough. Cut the hanging hook off and straighten it out with pliers.

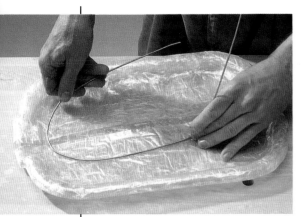 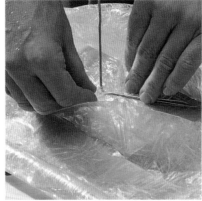 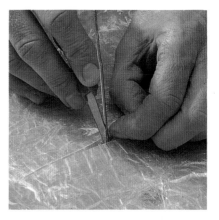

18 The final configurations of the sculpture means that the centre of gravity lies outside the cup and saucer. The cast of the tray is used to rectify this. The wire needs to be bent around so that a long part can fit inside one half of the tray. Keep one end of the wire vertical and at right angles to the piece being bent.

19 Securely tape this wire down to the interior bottom surface of the tray. Once the wire is securely fixed, press the two parts of the tray together and fold the flaps of the tray down. Fix it together with tape.

20 You will need to trim the clear tape around the area where the vertical piece of wire rises from the tray.

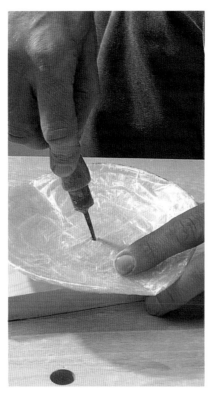

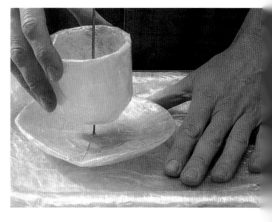

21 The wire is now fixed inside the tray. This is the main support structure for the rest of the sculpture. Since you are still able to see the bent wire inside the tray, you will need to build up more layers of tape on its top surface, making it more opaque to obscure the wire.

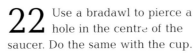

22 Use a bradawl to pierce a hole in the centre of the saucer. Do the same with the cup.

23 Now thread the saucer and cup onto the vertical wire. Tape each of them in place, making sure that the tape follows the form of the cup and saucer.

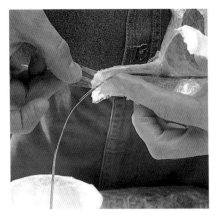 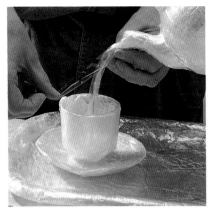

25 With the teapot now seemingly suspended in mid-air, proceed to cover the exposed wire with loosely-applied vertical pieces of tape. This will give the illusion of pouring liquid. Also add more tape, if necessary, to strengthen and increase the opaqueness of the casts to hide the wire support.

24 Bend the vertical wire round in a curve so that it overhangs the rest of the tray area. Place the half spout of the teapot (remember you did not fully join the two halves of the pot together) to the middle of the bent wire. Fix the wire securely inside the spout of the teapot. Once the wire is fixed inside, join the remainder of the pot together.

NARRATIVE

A NARRATIVE (STORY) can be
constructed within a sculpture and
this requires viewers to become
active participants for the sculpture
to be a success; they need to be
able to read the narrative arising
from the relationship between the
objects used in the sculpture.

Some sculptures may be
composed of only one form from
which the viewer is able to read a
particular sequence of events that
surround it, though this is
admittedly a more difficult type of
narrative sculpture. You will more
commonly find groups of more than
one object contained within the
sculpture and this makes it easier
to read the narrative.

The use of everyday objects has
become an important aspect of
making sculpture. Some sculptures
are composed wholly or in part of
everyday objects, requiring the
minimum of physical intervention
by the artist. In other sculptures a
cast of an object has been made,
without the sculptor having to form
the object in another material first.
A sense of narrative can be
invoked within the sculpture as
much by what is there as by what
is not there. It is interesting to
note how the figurative tradition
of sculpture is being continued
by taking a cast directly from
the figure.

▲ Laura DiMeo
UNCOVERED TORSO

This concrete torso was cast from a
plaster mould taken directly from the
artist's body. The result provides an
enigma for the viewer: who or what is it?
is it new or is it old? does it have a
history? It certainly has the appearance of
a fragment which might be seen in a
museum.
66 × 139 × 42 cm
(26 × 54¾ × 16½ in) with stand

▼ Robert Callender
LASTING IMPRESSIONS (DETAIL)

A relief sculpture of decaying objects,
made from painted card, wood and paper
pulp, have been arranged in a way
reminiscent of a museum display case.
122 × 61 cm (48 × 24 in)

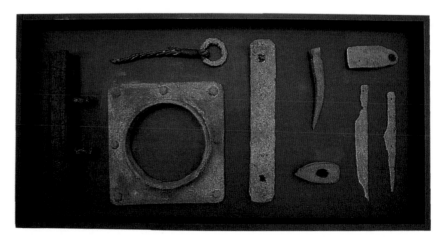

▼ Valerie Coffin Price
GENESIS

A relief sculpture which combines plaster
casts taken from the building and
collections at the Natural History
Museum, London. The fossils and
architectural decorations have been
painted to create a narrative.
152.5 × 110.5 × 5 cm (60 × 43½ × 2 in)

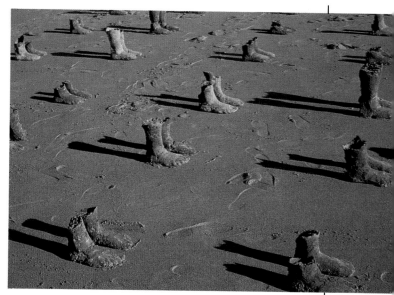

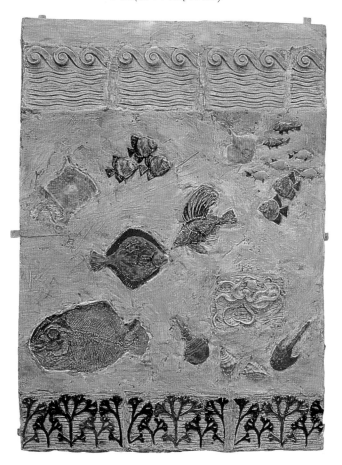

▲ Laura DiMeo
SILENT SOUNDS OF REPETITION (DETAIL)

These concrete casts of feet have been
used to produce a sculpture placed on a
beach; as the tide comes in they are
washed out to sea.
Feet are women's size 6

▼ Brian Ord
COW HEEL PIE

This wall-based sculpture composed of
real objects and forms made by the artist
constructs a narrative which deals with
the love-hate relationship the artist has
with domesticity.
*120 × 60 × 60 cm
(4 × 2 × 2 ft)*

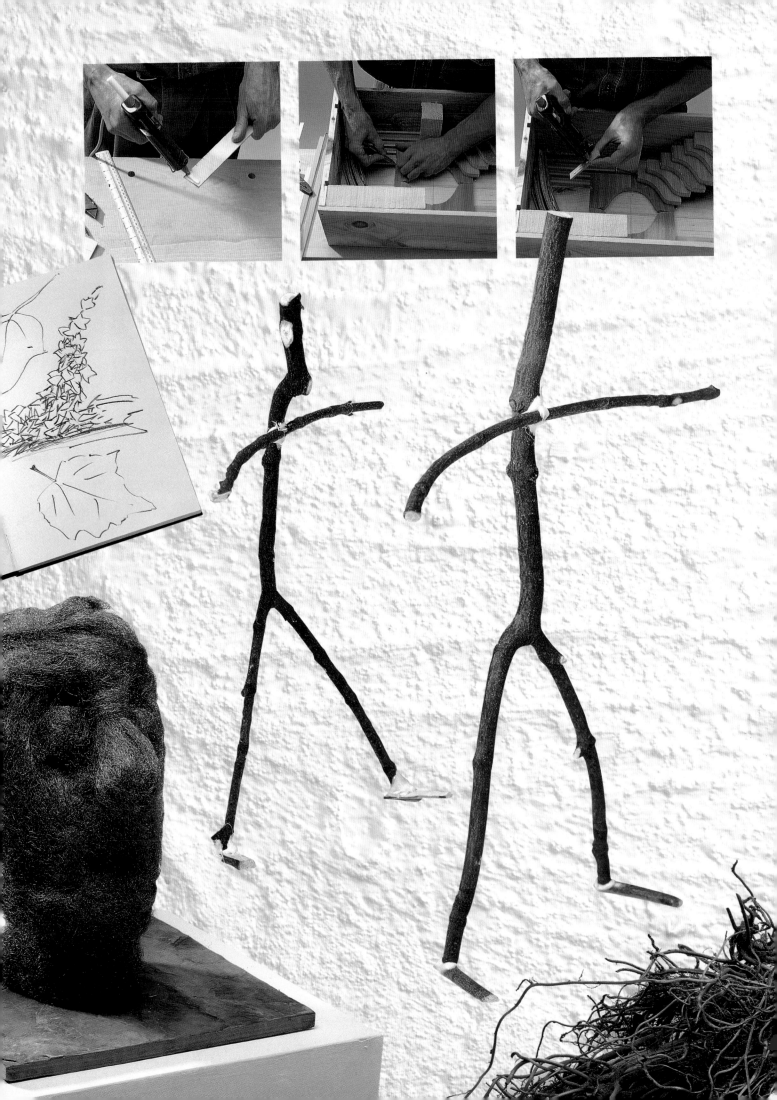

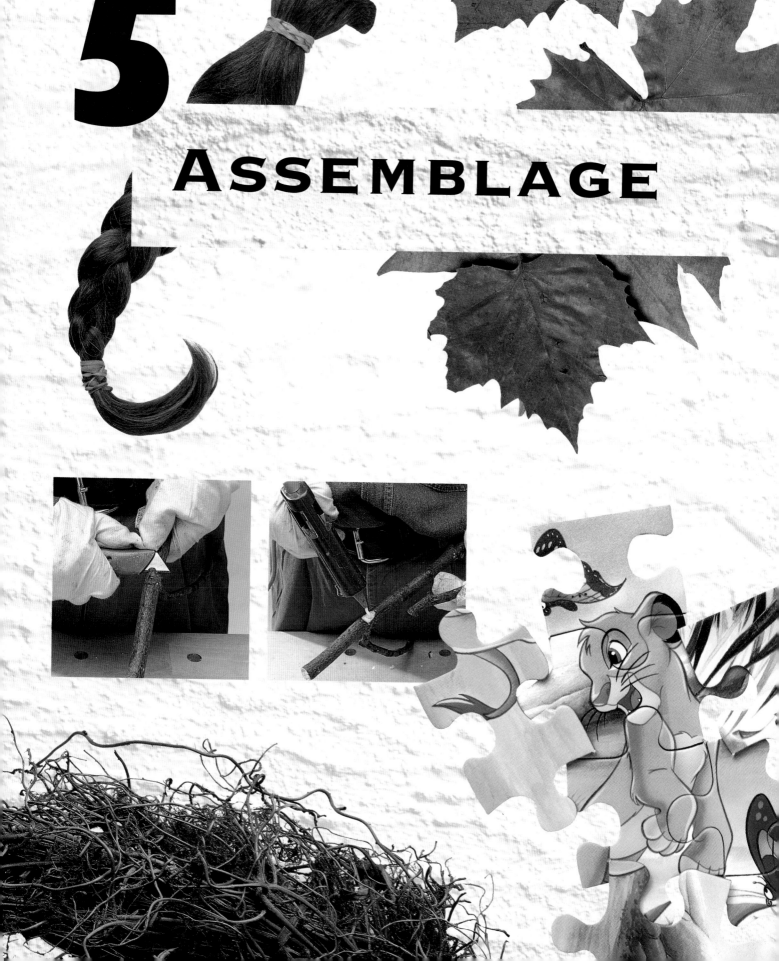

5 ASSEMBLAGE

COMPOSITION IN A BOX

▼ When creating a sculptural composition you constantly assess whether a piece looks right in a particular position, just as you would when doing a jigsaw puzzle.

A WORD ABOUT COMPOSITION. When applied to sculpture or any other visual art, it becomes an intimidating and difficult concept. However, there is no need for this to be so. Composition is something that everyone has knowledge of – something that we do subconsciously every day. For instance, when you look in a mirror and arrange your clothes or brush your hair until you are pleased with the result, you are composing yourself; a compositional decision has been made. When you arrange furniture in a room you are also making a compositional decision. You know when something looks right and when something does not.

In this project, you are making a composition in a defined space – the interior space of a box. You will be exploring the spatial facets of the box by making a composition from wood offcuts.

Before starting, just look around you. Find an arrangement of familiar things – say a bowl of fruit and candles on a table – and regroup them into a pleasant arrangement and then one that is not. You will notice that in any composition there is some sort of logic at work, a sense of order. Otherwise chaos reigns – the converse of composition.

Once all the wood offcuts are in place, paint the whole of the interior of the box one colour. This is an important compositional device used in sculpture, especially ones that are made from more than one part and more than one material. By applying paint to these disparate parts you visually pull the parts together into a coherent whole.

Although the project is about ordering and composing elements inside an interior space, it is also about seeing and evaluating visual possibilities, and acting on your instincts.

Materials

wooden box
wood offcuts
white spray paint
black paint (matt)
white spirit

Equipment

pencil
ruler
glue gun
wood glue sticks
masking tape
craft knife
paintbrush

Health/Safety

rubber gloves
respirator/dust mask
goggles

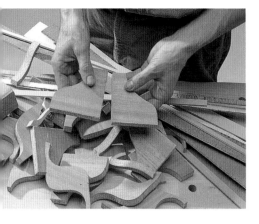

1 Ask a bottle store or fruit and vegetable shop if they have any wooden boxes. Alternatively, use an old drawer. Sort through wood offcuts to find interesting shapes and try to imagine how they might fit together.

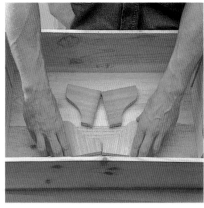

2 Having selected a variety of pieces – which in this case are the same shape – place them inside the box. Move them around in the space to find an interesting configuration to act as a starting point.

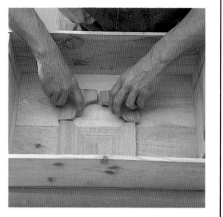

3 This is a good solution. Four shapes are arranged centrally in the box. Although the box is presently lying down on the bench, remember that it must stand vertically when the sculpture is complete.

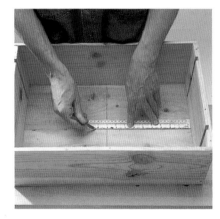

4 From the four sides of the box, measure and mark the centre point. Then draw a line through it from side to side.

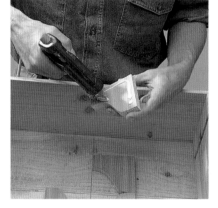

5 Using the glue gun, apply glue to the underside of each shape. Fix them firmly in place, using the lines you have drawn as your guide.

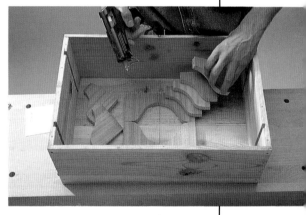

6 Using several offcuts of the same shape, create a stepped repetition up to one corner of the box. Take care that each shape is securely fixed in place before you move on to the next. Since only part of the underside of each shape is in contact with the shape beneath it, only apply glue to that contact point.

124

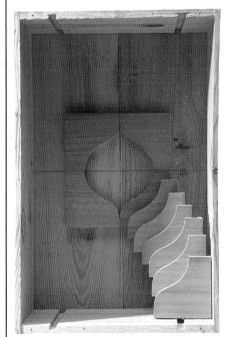

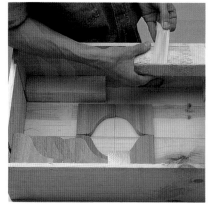

8 In order to assess further placement of offcuts, it is advisable to fix them in place first with masking tape, then position the box vertically to see if the composition works.

7 Working with the bottom of the box flat on the table makes it easier to glue the shapes in. It is absolutely essential, however, that after the parts have been added, you position the box vertically to look at the way the components complement one another and how they appear against the interior.

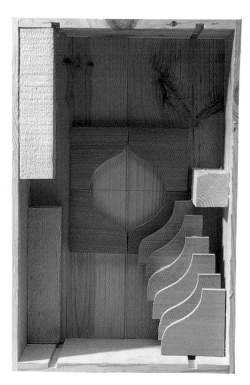

9 Three further pieces of timber have been fixed in place. Notice how their position to one another is determined by the centre point and by the depth of the box.

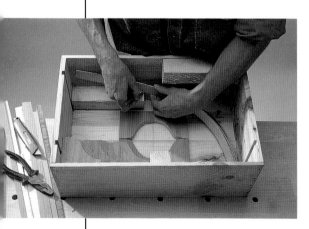

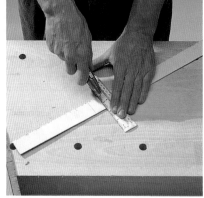

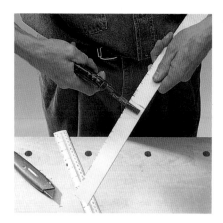

10 Among the offcuts were strips of very flexible plywood. They are useful to contribute some curves within the otherwise fairly straight symmetry of the box. The arcs will also echo the curves of the repeated shape that was first put in. Starting from one corner of the box, bend the strip around. Mark its positions on the end of the wood block.

11 Place a straight edge along this mark and cut the plywood a couple of times with your craft knife.

12 There is no need to cut all the way through the plywood with the knife. Grip the unneeded part of wood along the cut line; the wood will snap off.

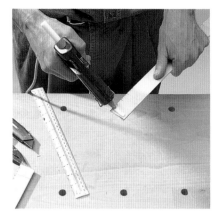
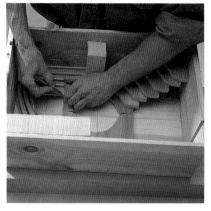
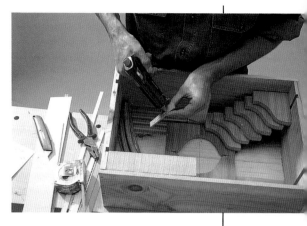

13 Now position and glue the plywood curve into the box. This is best done by applying glue to each end of the strip and quickly sticking one end in one corner of the box, then bending the strip and gluing the other end in place, working quickly so that the operation is done before the glue sets.

14 Now place strips of MDF wood in the area between the curves and the repeated shapes. Hold a strip in position, then remove it and mark where it needs to be cut, doing this in the same way as the plywood.

15 All these strips must be glued in position as you go along. Alternate the faces of the wood strips which you glue to the box.

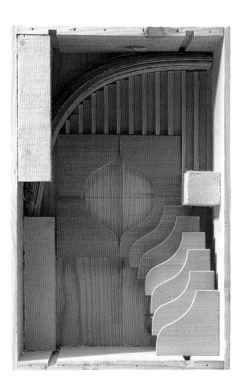

16 The overall composition is taking shape. The curved wood draws attention to the top enclosed corner area, at the same time efficiently containing the vertical strips of wood. The repeat step shapes and the blocks draw the eye into the centre.

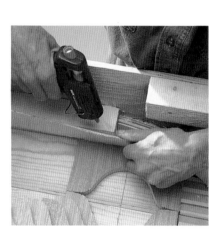

17 Cut, bend and glue two wider strips of plywood into position.

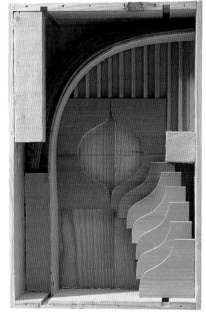

18 The last two pieces of plywood link the bottom of the box to the top while continuing the contrast between straight and curved lines.

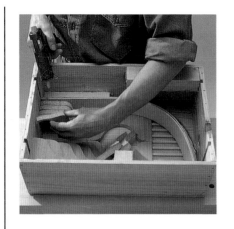

19 Fill the empty space at the bottom of the box with repeated shapes. Coat one side with glue and abut one against another.

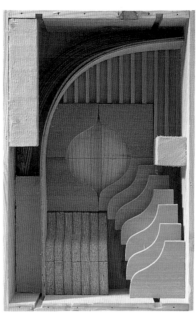

20 The composition is now more of a whole; the individual pieces combine to produce one form.

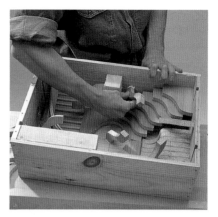

21 As a final compositional element glue these wiggly shapes into the box. Their ends reach out and explore the space inside the box.

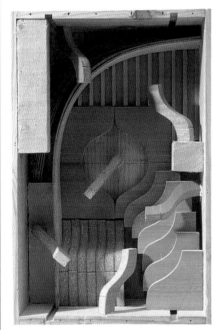

22 The fixing of the wooden parts is now finished. The composition is almost complete. But the individual identity of each part is still obvious. Applying paint to the interior will visually unite these parts into a coherent whole. Painting the outside of the box a darker colour will reinforce the fact that the box is both container and frame.

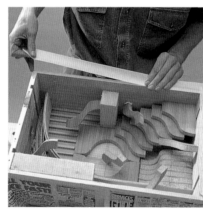

23 Cover the top edges of the box with masking tape and put newspaper around the sides of the box. Hold the paper in place with tape.

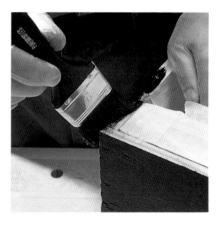

24 Wear rubber gloves, a face mask and goggles for spraying the interior of the box white. Make sure that the paint reaches into all the nooks and crannies. Once the paint inside is dry, mask the interior of the box with tape. Paint the top edges, sides and back of the box with black paint. Clean your brush with white spirit.

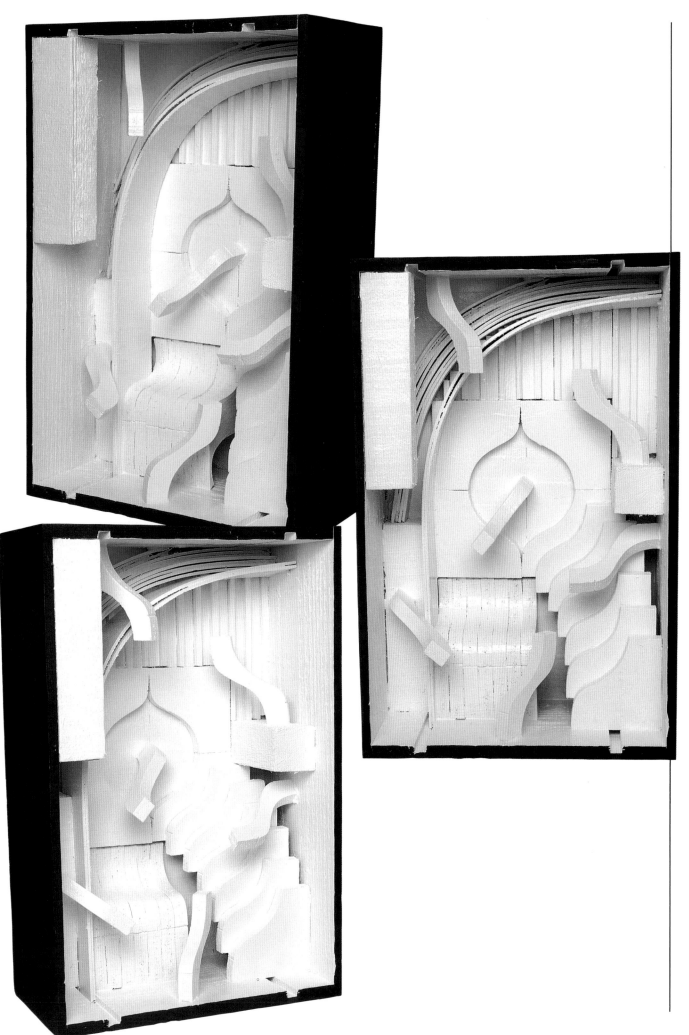

AUTUMN LEAVES

USING A REPEATED form in a sculpture, means that you can concentrate on the relationship these forms have with one another rather than on the form itself. The aim is to produce a coherent composition which gives a sense of movement within the sculpture.

The inspiration for this project came from a walk in a local park in autumn, when the ground was covered in fallen leaves. Some were overlaid on one another in heaps, but since it was windy other leaves were blown into the air. Excited by the sculptural possibilities, I made drawings of the windswept leaves; then at a later stage I made further developmental drawings with a potential sculpture in mind.

As you have already discovered in projects like "Composition in a Box" (see pp. 122–7), recycled material can be ideal for sculptural purposes. Here, drink cans offer a bountiful supply of thin metal sheets which are easily cut, shaped and fixed. Once a leaf shape has been cut, it can be curled and bent to imitate a leaf. When deciding on the leaf shape, it is important to ensure that its size will fit within the dimensions of a flattened-out drink can, and that you are able to get the maximum number from each sheet. When the sculpture is finished, spray the entire work with red oxide paint to unify the composition and to reinforce that autumnal feeling.

▲ If you always carry a sketchbook, you can make an instant record of objects or events that present sculptural possibilities for you.

▲ Collect a variety of leaves and then draw them individually with the aim of obtaining a stylized leaf shape that will suit a sculpture.

Materials

empty drink cans
card
red oxide spray paint

Equipment

pencil
craft knife
scissors
glue gun
all-purpose glue sticks

Health/Safety

canvas gloves
rubber gloves
respirator mask

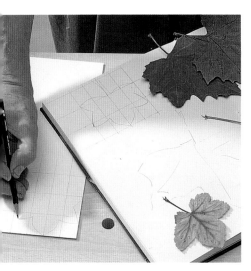

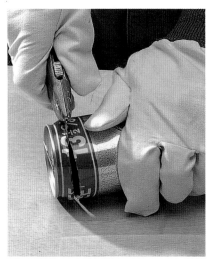

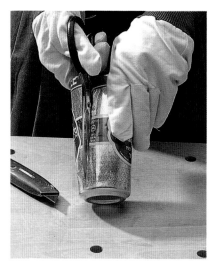

1 Collect some appealing fallen leaves and make drawings of them in your sketchbook. From these drawings you will need to develop a stylized leaf shape of a size which will fit onto a flattened-out drink can. Once decided upon, redraw the leaf on a piece of card and cut it out. This is your template, to be used when cutting shapes from the metal.

2 Wear gloves for protection against accidental slippage of the craft knife and the sharp edges of the can. Pierce the can on its side near the top, then begin cutting off the top of the can by slowly drawing the knife toward you, while at the same time rotating the can away from you with your other hand.

3 Use scissors to cut along the length of the can to the base.

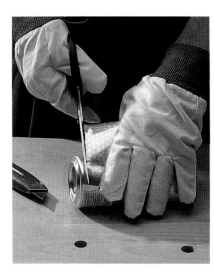

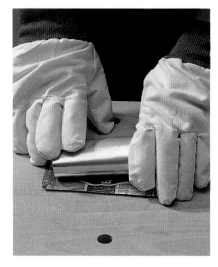

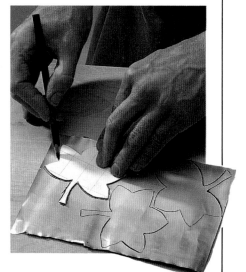

4 When you reach the base of the can, turn the scissors at right angles to the line you have just cut and cut off the base of the can.

5 To flatten the sheet out, place the metal can on the bench, straighten it out and then roll it up in the opposite direction to its former shape. Once this is done the sheet will lie more or less flat.

6 Position your card template on the sheet several times until you have discovered the best way to obtain the maximum number of leaf shapes from each sheet. Draw round the leaf shape with a pencil.

Safety

- **Wear gloves for protection when cutting the leaf shapes**
- **Use spray paint outdoors or in a well ventilated area**
- **Wear rubber gloves and a respirator mask**
- **Make sure all surrounding areas are covered with paper**

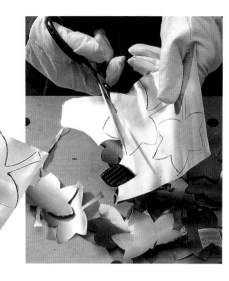

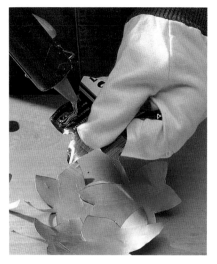

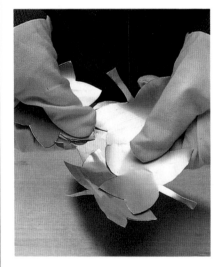

7 As you can see, I was able to fit three leaf shapes onto this sheet of metal. Don't worry if the sheet is not completely flat; it doesn't really matter since leaves themselves will be rolled up and twisted.

8 Once you have marked out leaves on several sheets, use scissors to cut around the shapes. Cut out too many rather than too few leaves.

9 Your first task is to create a solid mass of leaf shapes. Do this by applying glue to the printed side of the metal.

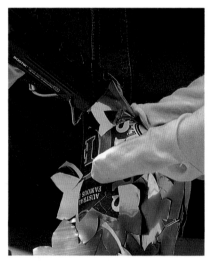

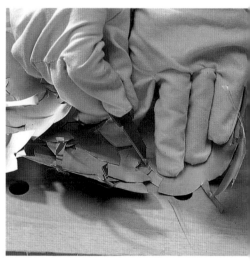

10 Quickly press one leaf on another and hold it there tightly and firmly for a few moments until the glue from the gun has set. Always wear gloves when doing this because the metal will get hot from the hot glue. Also remember to work speedily and efficiently, since the glue cools and sets quickly.

11 As you build up your mass of leaves, give it added strength by applying glue between gaps in the overlapping leaf shapes.

12 Squeeze excess glue from between the leaves and trim it off with a small modelling knife.

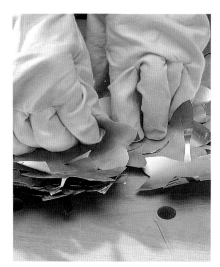

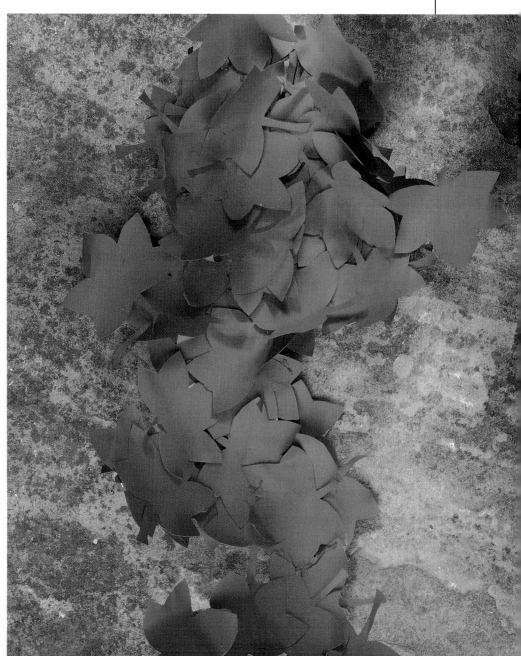

14 The construction of the sculpture is now complete. The lightness of the material, combined with the speed and efficiency of the glue gun, has allowed you to position the leaves in quite precarious positions, emphasizing the movement of rustling leaves.

13 Now your mass of leaf shapes are glued in place. To emphasize the look of a windblown pile of leaves, curl and bend individual leaf shapes, taking care not to pull the leaves away from their fixing.

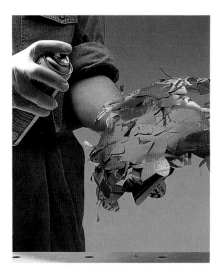

15 To highlight that autumnal aspect of the sculpture, spray the whole thing with an appropriate colour – in this case red oxide car spray. Mask all surrounding areas with newspaper first.

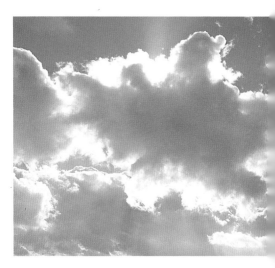

TWIG FIGURES

THERE IS AN imaginative aspect of perception which most, if not all, of us have experienced at some time or another. That is the ability to visualize images and scenes when looking into the flames of a fire, at the folds in drapery, up at the clouds or even at the cracks and blemishes on walls or floors. In fact, certain situations elicit a consensus about the type of images that are conjured up. An example can be found in the undulating curves of a hilly landscape – often used as a metaphor for the human form. This visual suggestibility should be encouraged in all artists – indeed, an artist has the ability to find inspiration and stimulus where others would see nothing. It is this talent – and skill – that is addressed in this project.

Trees, because of their upright stance and the linear form of their twigs and branches, possess definite figurative connotations. For this sculpture you use only small branches and twigs collected around recently pruned or felled trees – don't damage trees unnecessarily. Assemble a collection of random twig shapes, sizes and lengths, and select those pieces which you feel instinctively will contribute to a successful figurative sculpture. You are limited by the natural configuration of the twigs in your attempt to convey a figurative message, so choose carefully and do not pick too many pieces. Join the twigs together using a glue gun.

The only physical limit on your imaginative enthusiasm is that the pieces must be joined so that the sculpture maintains its balance and does not fall over.

◀ Ordinary objects can conjure up images when viewed imaginatively. A simple twig broom has figurative connotations.

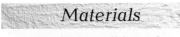

Materials

twigs and small branches

Equipment

secateurs
G-clamp
tenon saw
craft knife
old kitchen knife
glue gun
all-purpose glue stick

Health/Safety

canvas gloves

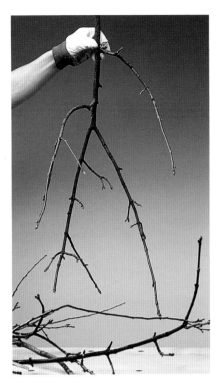

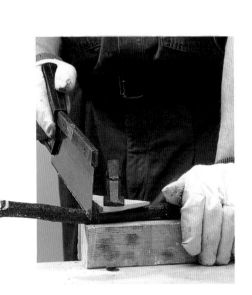

1 Sort through the pile of twigs and branches, selecting those with the most figurative connotations.

2 Use secateurs to trim off unwanted lengths.

3 When trimming the thicker pieces, hold them securely in place with a G-clamp, inserting a piece of architrave moulding in between the clamp and the branch to ensure a firm grip.

4 Use a tenon saw to cut the end off.

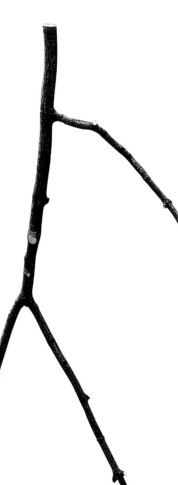

5 The branch has been ▷ trimmed and cut down to produce a good starting point for a figure. It will require only a minimum of extra material to be added.

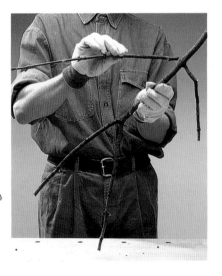

6 Try adding another small branch to see if it provides an adequate match for the one already there.

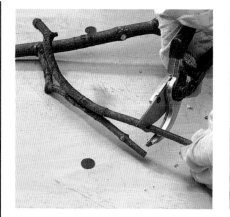

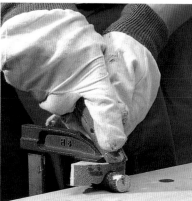

8 Clamp a short length to the ◀ bench, using the architrave moulding as before. Insert the blade of a craft knife into the top end of the wood. Gently wiggle the knife back and forth to open up a crack. Insert an old kitchen knife into this crack, move it from side to side, and you will find that the wood will split along its length.

7 Use secateurs to cut this small branch to the same length as the other.

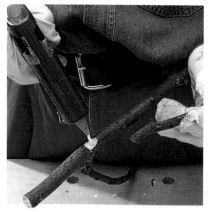

9 The original branch together with a length for the arm, and two split lengths for the feet.

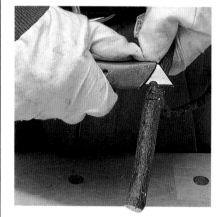

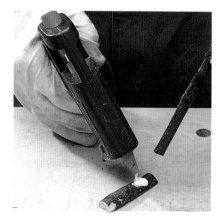

10 Cut away an area of bark off the main body where the arm will be fixed.

11 Apply glue to the "body" and firmly push the arm into place. Once set, trim off any excess glue with a craft knife.

12 Strip an area of bark off the foot. Apply glue and push the leg firmly into place. Position the leg on the foot so that the figure can stand up without falling over.

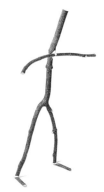

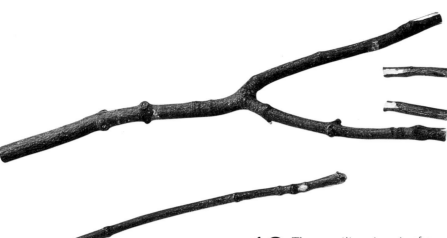

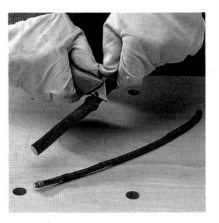

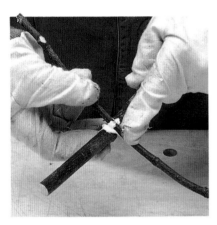

13 The constituent parts of a smaller figure. There are no arms growing on the main branch, so a longer length is necessary in order to make arms by crossing over the vertical main branch.

14 Strip the bark off the main branch where the arms will be fixed. Strip off an area of bark at the midway point on the twig which will be the arms.

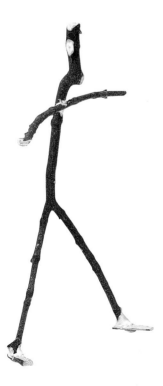

15 Apply glue to the main branch and push the arms firmly into place, positioning them centrally on the main branch.

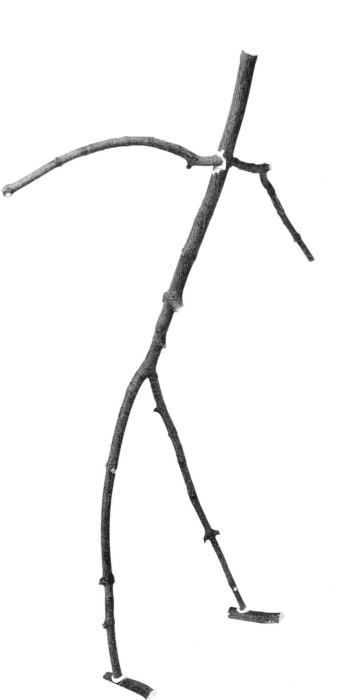

IMAGINARY HEAD

WHETHER YOU ARE carving, modelling, constructing or making an assemblage sculpture, in the final analysis it is the material that determines the form your sculpture takes. It cannot be emphasized enough that you must have a full understanding of the possibilities and limitations of your material, and show respect for it by exploiting its potential to the full.

The only way to really find out about a material is by working with it, pushing it around to see what it can and cannot do. Invariably this process will have a determining effect on the final form. In this project you use ordinary wire wool. Because it is not a material usually associated with sculpture, it carries no burden of expectation and you are free to use it in any way you like.

I began by making drawings, keeping the pencil on the paper as in automatic drawing, creating a mass of interweaving pencil lines. From this chaos a head evolved. As a result, this project will take the form of a head. It is not a portrait head or at all recognizable, but rather an imaginary one.

In the same way that the form of the drawn head was determined by the automatic pencil marks, so the form which the sculpture will take depends on the process employed in shaping the wire wool. The material must have an inherent structural strength to enable it to stand up. That is why a plaiting technique is used – the same method used with hair or wool. This renders strands a lot tougher and, by coiling the plaited lengths on top of one another, allows you to achieve the necessary strong vertical structure.

▼ Begin by making drawings, keeping the pencil on the paper as in automatic drawing, creating a mass of interweaving pencil lines. From this chaos shapes may evolve.

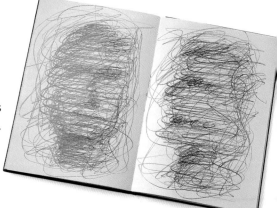

◄ This wreath is an excellent example of the way chaos and order can co-exist.

Materials

wire wool

Equipment

sketch pad
pencil/pen
scissors

Health/Safety

rubber gloves

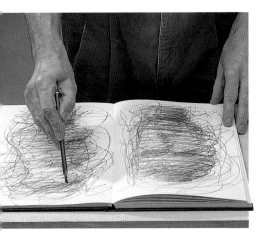

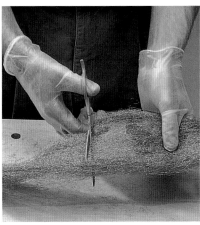

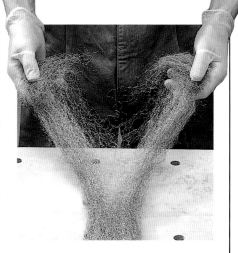

1 Cover your sheet with pencil marks, keeping the pencil moving around the sheet and developing the form of a head.

2 Use scissors to cut a length of wire wool approximately 75 cm (30 in) from the roll.

3 Pull the wire wool apart to create two separate strands of even thickness. Make several such strands.

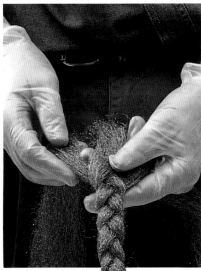

4 Take three of these strands of wire wool and plait them in the same way as one would plait hair.

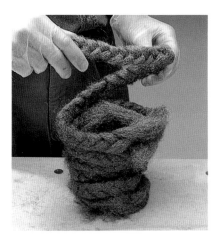

5 There is no need to tie the end of each plait up. Simply push each end together and the nature of the material will hold it in place, preventing the plait from unravelling. ▼

6 Coil the plaits around, placing the plaited lengths on top of one another to create a small cylindrical shape. This will become the neck.

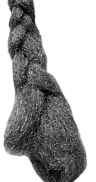

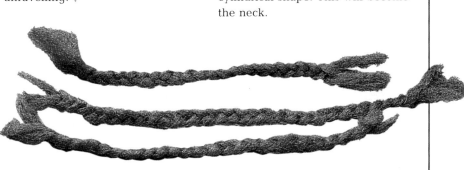

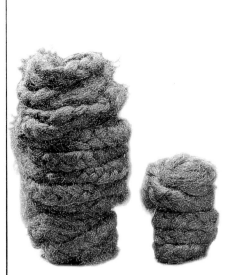

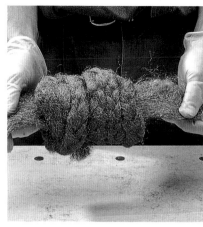

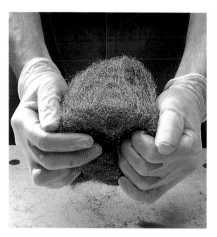

7 Make more wire wool plaits and coil them round to create a cylinder that is taller and has a larger diameter. This is the head, seen here with the neck.

8 Cut off a length of wire wool and insert it into the centre of the neck. Pull the wire wool length out at either end to increase the width and breadth of the neck.

9 Wrap each end of the wire length over the front surface of the cylinder. Tuck the ends into the inside of the cylinder, keeping the wire wool as taut as possible.

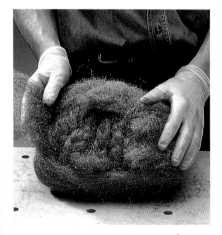

10 Do the same with the head section, inserting lengths inside the cylinder and wrapping them around as above, until the coiled plaits are completely covered.

11 The neck and head sections have now assumed a recognizable form. The wire wool wrapped around the coiled plaits holds them firmly in place, producing two sturdy structures. ▼

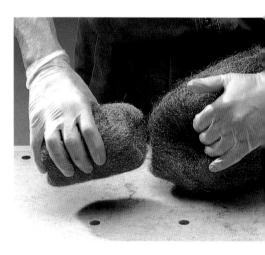

12 Gently hold open one end of the head section, squeeze the neck section together in the other hand, and push it in halfway into the head section.

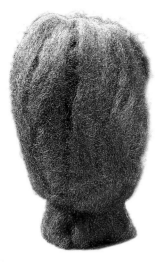 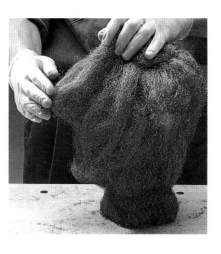 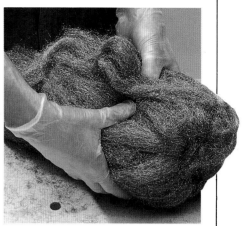

13 You now have a sculpture in the form of a head that is able to stand up by itself.

14 Accentuate the shape of the side profile, adding some wire wool for the nose. Tuck the extra wire wool into the head's surface – you will find that it stays there.

15 Now that the basic side profile is developed, you can start to shape the front of the head. Lie the head down and push in either side of the nose to create the eye sockets. Twist, squeeze and tuck in these two areas of wire wool.

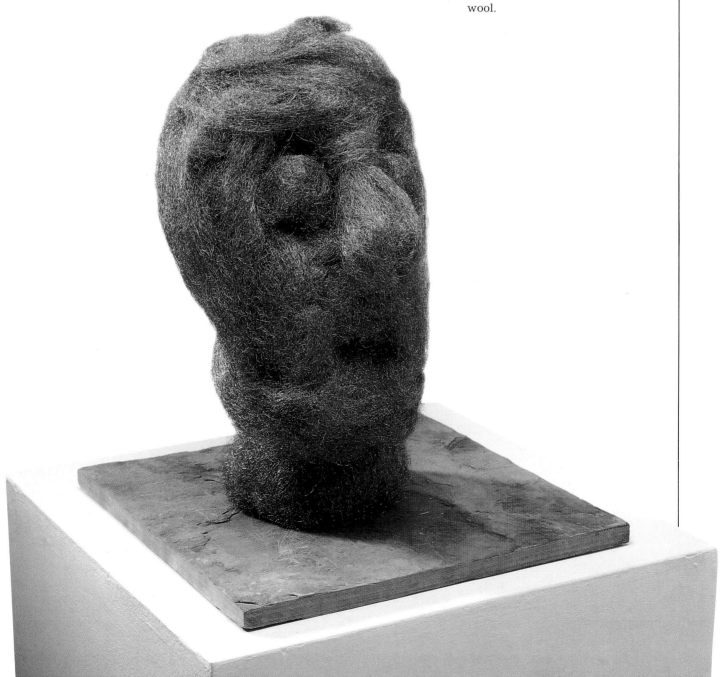

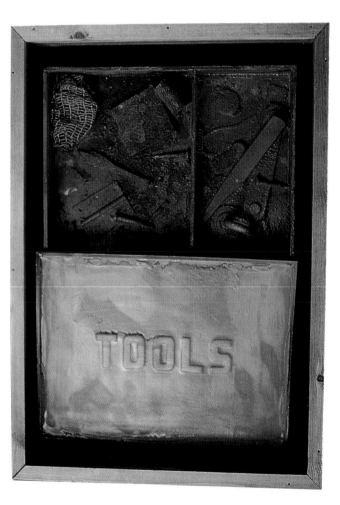

CONTEXT

FINDING A STARTING POINT for a piece of sculpture can at times be an uphill struggle. One way to overcome this problem is to provide a context from the outset within which to make the sculpture. For instance, this could mean making a sculpture in a box or on a wall; of predetermined dimensions; or limiting the amount and/or type of material used etc.

Setting a context in this way creates a starting point for making a sculpture. This in turn will hopefully also act as a catalyst and generate more exciting forms and sculptural configurations. In addition, providing such a context makes it a lot easier for the viewer to appreciate and understand the sculpture. The sculptures shown in this section all relied on having a context within which they were made; consequently this also provides the context in which they are viewed.

▼ **Robert Callender**
TOOLS 1994

The format of a box has been used to set the context for this sculpture. A tool box and contents have been constructed using painted card and paper placed within a wooden box.
61 × 40 cm (24 × 15¾ in)

▲ **Hilary Bryanston**
THE GOLDEN FISH

The weird and wonderful shapes found in branches provided the inspiration for this sculpture. Some parts of the wood have been left in their natural shape while other areas have been carved, leaving tool marks, and painted gold.
81.5 × 30.5 × 23 cm
(32 × 12 × 9 in)

▶ Sophie Ryder
ROCKING AND ROLLING

This is an example of a repeated shape being put to good use in a sculpture. Profiles of a bird in flight cut from steel and then welded and pegged together have produced a real sense of movement within the sculpture, encapsulating a sense of bird flight.

4.6 × 9.1 m (15 × 30 ft)

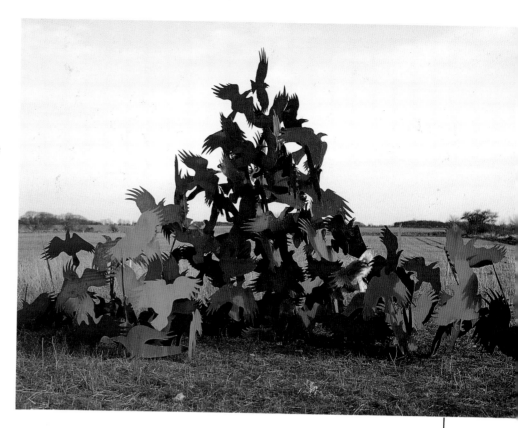

▼ David Heathcote
LIMESTONE HEAD

Using a head as the context to make a sculpture can prove to be a fruitful avenue to explore. It allows you to sculpt a head from your imagination or, as in this case, be influenced by the art of another culture.

45 cm (17 in)

▶ Brian Yale
THE DUNGENESS DRIFTER

By bringing together diverse found objects and pieces of timber washed up by the sea the artist has created a figurative sculpture which exudes a real sense of humour.

40.5 cm (16 in)

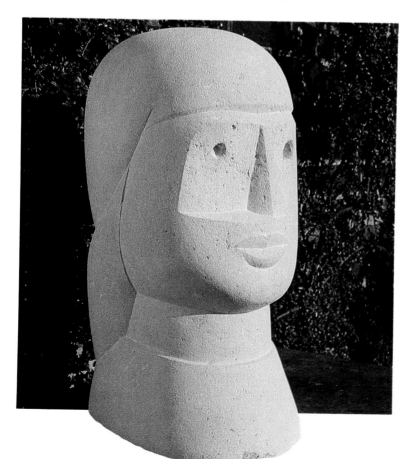

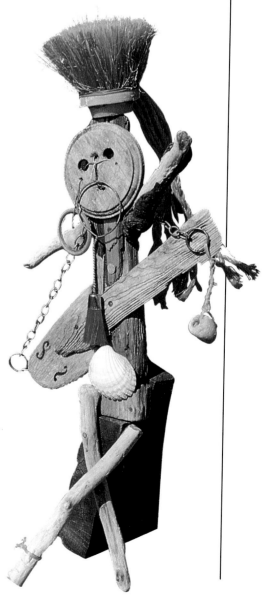

INDEX

All projects and techniques are illustrated. Page numbers in *italics* refer to illustrations separated from appropriate text.

143

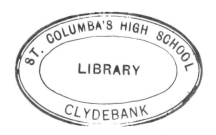

ACKNOWLEDGEMENTS

The author would like to dedicate this book to Billy.

The author would also like to thank Eve Khambatta fo her assistance in the studio, and Nicola Streeten for her continuing support and encouragement.

Quarto Publishing would like to thank all the sculptors who submitted finished work for this book and the following people who supplied photographs: **36 below left** Ace Photo Agency; **42 below left and right** from *Illustrator's Figure Reference Manual*; **48 top right and middle** from *Illustrator's Figure Reference Manual*; **54 right** from *Encyclopedia of Dog Breeds*; **64 bottom** Ace Photo Agency; **68 top right and middle right** from *How to Draw and Paint Textures*, **below left** Moira Clinch; **74 right** 8176 Trek 95 Hanson/Dodge; **100 middle left** Moira Clinch; **106 below left** from *Illustrator's Nudes Reference Manual*; **132 right** Moira Clinch

Index by Dorothy Frame